Embodied Inquiry

Embodied Inquiry

Writing, Living and Being through the Body

Celeste Snowber
Simon Fraser University, Canada

SENSE PUBLISHERS
ROTTERDAM/BOSTON/TAIPEI

A C.I.P. record for this book is available from the Library of Congress.

ISBN: 978-94-6300-753-5 (paperback)
ISBN: 978-94-6300-754-2 (hardback)
ISBN: 978-94-6300-755-9 (e-book)

Published by: Sense Publishers,
P.O. Box 21858,
3001 AW Rotterdam,
The Netherlands
https://www.sensepublishers.com/

All chapters in this book have undergone peer review.

Cover image: *Parpallo IV*, by Mary Blaze (http://blazeworksstudio.com/)

Printed on acid-free paper

ADVANCE PRAISE FOR
EMBODIED INQUIRY

"More than an instruction manual or a hands-on guide, this valuable book is a call to re-inhabit our most precious and essential bodies. When read with full-spectrum vision, it will enliven scholarship and transform daily habits in ways that improve life quality and mobilize creativity. Celeste guides us across multiple thresholds, coming ever closer to embodied wisdom in ways that transcend categories, disciplines and old habits of thought. Her book inspires me to live more fully with its heartfelt call to re-engage the only body I will ever have in this singular life. I recommend it wholeheartedly."
– **Michelle LeBaron, B.A. J.D. M.A., Professor and dispute resolution scholar | Peter A. Allard School of Law, University of British Columbia, Editor of *The Choreography of Resolution: Conflict, Movement and Neuroscience***

"Weaving prose and poetry, Snowber awakens our sensual and embodied self at the very roots of living. She invites us to mindfully listen to our body and to follow its leads into the act of knowing and writing. Not wishing to settle for a separate methodology her proposal is bold: embodied practices can infuse all forms of inquiry. This deeply personal work will move educators, researchers, artists, and those for whom lived experience is core to their creative process."
– **Daniel Deslauriers, Ph.D., Professor, Transformative Studies Doctorate Program California Institute of Integral Studies**

"Before I met Celeste Snowber (through various publication projects), I had distanced myself from being a mother – or rather, my children belonged to my private life – and not seen or heard in my professional life. Reading Celeste's work over a number of years now, I have been encouraged (and at first went unwillingly) to feel and share my children in my writing, teaching and editing life. Celeste writes, 'you have been trained how to read and write. I am calling you back to a place where blood turns to ink, and flesh seeps into your words so they sing and pulse off the page'. Celeste's work has changed me: it has challenged me too. Her work is political and feminist, but this book 'is not a new fancy methodology', but rather 'an invocation to bring aspects to our lives which will infuse our vocation, creativity and research'. The body is not left behind, lonely and silenced in Celeste's writing – the book grows out of our humanness: paradox, pain, suffering and our inescapable embodied life-journey. In this way, Celeste's book is existential. Giving our cells phenomenological time, takes up clock time, and she calls me into lived time – into feeling-full time. Encouraging embodied phenomenal feeling-time, to take time, in patriarchal institutions is Celeste's gift to us. In this

book Celeste gives organic voice to the lonely body, often unable to breathe and stretch-out in professions and vocations. Celeste's book deepens her previous work, and at times, is uncomfortable and challenging – in fact this book requires courage – because to be with feeling-full body, as Celeste points out, affects our ethics and decision making, and calls us into depths often unshared. Celeste writes a love poem from the body and I am called by my own body's sadness – my body is re/membered. Celeste's book is also phenomenological, where the body and its 'mores' are languaged into presence. In kinship with the phenomenological tradition, she attends to depth- language, where the body is not left behind in language-formulation."
– Amanda Williamson, Principal Editor of *The Journal of Dance, Movement and Spiritualities*, Honorary Professor C-dare, Coventry University

"'You do not *have* a body. You *are* a body.' With this assertion, Celeste Snowber invites you on a poetic exploration of the centrality of your physical self—your cells, blood, organs, and senses—to passionate, soulful living. Drawing upon her years of teaching, writing and dancing, she brings to life your body's role in making key life decisions, connecting with your creative muse, drawing upon your inherent insights and wisdom, and viewing your longings as thresholds for discovery.

Her lyrical prose, enriched by her luscious Bodypsalms, dances off the page as she feeds us story after story of how her body has nurtured an ecstatic approach to daily life. Her examples tantalize us into action. You may interrupt your reading of *Embodied Inquiry* to meander along a river bank, get down on the floor to play with children, savor luscious vegetables as you prepare supper, and capture a poem wafting up inside as you watch the birds.

Only one caveat: after imbibing this guide to embodied living, you and your body (and now your friend) will feel more alive, more engaged, more adventurous, and more grateful for your new relationship."
– Diane Glass, author of *This Need to Dance: A Life of Rhythm and Resilience*, co-founder of "Tending Your Inner Garden®"

"Poetic, passionate, purposeful! In an efficient, fast-paced, technological world, Celeste, with humour and honour, will stretch you to re-see what you have forgotten; the presence, joy, and wisdom of your body as a place of connecting you to your meaningful life!"
– Mary Beth Cancienne, Ph.D., Associate Professor, James Madison University

"When was the last time you took a moment to laze on your back and marvel at the glorious sky? Or took a moment to simply breathe? Or sensed what lives in your gut as you write or spend time with others? No matter where you may be or what you might be doing, Celeste's prose will inspire you to live more deeply within your body. From savoring moments of intense pleasure or passion to attuning to the pain that lives within heartache or injury, Celeste invites us to courageously dwell in the fullness of our vulnerabilities. And in taking Celeste's advice, to live each day with an embodied sense of inquiry, we may co-create a better existence, become more awake and alive, and experience all that there is to sense as we go forward, bodyward, heartward and soulward with no bounds."

Rebecca Lloyd, Ph.D., dancer, writer and Associate Professor in the Faculty of Education at the University of Ottawa

for my students
over the last few decades
who have dared to go on the journey
to call the body home

TABLE OF CONTENTS

PREFACE

> migrate to the life
> that wants to be lived in you
> one step at a time

Embodied Inquiry is offered to all of you who want to deepen your relationship and connection to your bodies. To deepen the relationship and connection to your body is to call forth the natural resource of living and being in the world. The body has a language of its own. The body calls to you continuously, the body wants its subtle notes and bold proclamations to be listened to and honoured. This process of the body communicating with you could be likened to a kayaker gliding on the water. The body is a riparian zone, 80% of a baby's body is water, and 60% of an adult's body is water. Like water, the body is delicate and strong at the same time. The body, like water, calls to you to flow and cooperate with your own nature.

For too long the body has been looked at as an object, as if from the outside. The body has been colonized, gendered, politicized, medicalized and consumerized. We have for too long bullied the body to look a certain way, be a certain way, or act a certain way. How the body is perceived has a direct relationship to the ability to disconnect from the body's knowledge and wisdom. What would it mean to live from the inside out? To take back the body, to refuse its objectification is to restore the body to its status of natural habitat. When we are comfortable in our own skins, we are able to celebrate the beautiful, paradoxical site where limitations and joy dwell together.

In this book, I invite you to see the body as a place of inquiry, a place of learning, understanding and perceiving. All of the knowledge of how to listen to the body is already within you. Following the innate knowledge of the body is the ultimate way of being. The body wants to woo you back to yourself, where the voice within your belly and skin has prominence. There is a time to say yes to the grammar of the gut. Listening to the body can be as sweet as a concerto. I invite you to listen to your own birdsong.

Listening to the body is as valuable and its physicality is as integral to our lives as listening to spiritual, philosophical or intellectual guidance. From a visceral perspective, spirituality and physicality are deeply entwined and interwoven in the fabric of our cells. Coming to knowledge and understanding of what it means to listen to the body is necessary for all who want to access a holistic and healthy path. Whether you are a scientist or artist, lawyer or educator, performer or poet, administrator or physician, you can benefit from a more fully embodied engagement to your life. This book is an invitation to bring the possibilities of how our senses and bodily ways of perceiving and understanding can inform our personal and professional lives.

This approach is not new nor does it represent new knowledge. This knowledge comes from the ancients, the wise ones, the indigenous people and the mystics. You've heard it. You know it. That's because this knowledge is as earthly as the gardener's hands. I am one of those gardeners, whose fingers write from the earth. My words are what I grow. This book comes out of decades of teaching, writing and researching particularly in the area of bringing embodied ways of inquiry to arts education. My scholarship has also led me to bring embodied inquiry to pedagogy, transforming my teaching and students' ways of learning and opening up embodied ways of inquiry within curriculum studies and arts-based research. Many years ago, when I began my study and research in embodiment, both as a dancer and scholar, I was struck by how disembodied the discourse on the body actually was. Scholars spoke of embodiment and the body as if it was a linear text, and of the body as if it didn't blush, pale, weep or sweat. This dialogue and approach was radically different from the life I was leading as a dance artist and mother of three small children.

Over the years I have sought to find ways to show undergraduate and graduate students the incredible resource of their bodies, valuable for their scholarship, practice, teaching and living. In this pursuit, I have found no one text or field adequate. Instead I learned what's valuable and developed my sensibility by reading broadly and drawing wisdom from a variety of fields, including poetics, curriculum studies, phenomenology, arts-based research, deep ecology, feminist studies and of course, from the experiences of daily life. This book is a companion piece to the vast scholarly work done on embodied ways of knowing and inquiry. May you take this along in your journey and be encouraged that all of life is connected to research, vocation, and how we live in our professions.

This book is an invitation to bring the possibilities of how our senses and bodily ways of perceiving and understanding can inform our personal and professional lives. The personal and universal are deeply connected and it has always been my intention to bring together the public and private, political and poetic, therefore my scholarly and creative work is grounded in the lived curriculum and garden of autobiography. This is the garden where stories have the ability to utter one another. We are found in each other's stories, whether they are written, oral, danced, painted or poeticized. My invitation to you is to let out your own stories, gestures, and bodily understandings be a place to co-create a better world. This book is peppered with my own autobiographical, lived experience as a way to usher you into reclaiming the potency of your own beautiful and paradoxical lives. The body is rooted in breath, rhythm and poetry and this book leans to a poetic exploration of embodiment. Haikus, poems and language rooted in the senses are part of its offering.

I have been hesitant over the years to create a name or methodology for this kind of work even though it has found voice within the fields of arts-based research and curriculum studies. These fields and their intersection with qualitative research, have opened up inquiry that values the phenomenological, the autobiographical, and the artistic. Arts-based research has burgeoned to live in a multiplicity of ways including poetic inquiry, artography, performative inquiry, arts-informed learning, and many more. What I have to offer is more of a way of being in the world, and can contribute to all of forms of inquiry. This is an embodied inquiry, which enriches all the methodologies of research and practice. There is not one plan, method, or form to follow. Instead, there is an invitation to live through your body and to be open and opened by experience.

I work and live from the premise that physicality, poetics and creativity are deeply intertwined. A return to celebration of our physicality awakens the juices of a creative life. Life in and of itself is an art form and living artfully and aesthetically is central to being responsive to a life. The body in all its fullness is a gift that allows us to walk, run, flop and fall along the journey that is set before us. This is the journey of being open to all of life, its mystery and despair, the ecstasy and sensual. And this ecstatic life is also one, which is open to our tears, for they are prayers, and the moisture needed for all joy to grow.

It is my hope that this book will infuse you with courage to live more deeply from what you already know in your body. May you call your body back to listen to the tenderness and wildness and everything else in between. May you have the courage to live in such a way that you are at home in your own skin. Of course this is not a one-time event, taking place after you read this book. This is truly a life practice.

With that, more than guidelines, I offer *Embodied Inquiry* as inspiration. It is a book designed to be picked up and put down, to sip in small doses. A few sentences to bring you back to the sentences that your body wants to write. There are intentionally recurrent themes as waves upon the shore. What you bring to this book in your own lived experience is vitally important. In this way reading is a co-creation. Through its words and your presence, may you connect to the deep knowledge and wisdom of your own body, and may you acknowledge it as the always present map within. A map to your own pilgrimage back to befriending your body. Again, you already know within you all of what I have to say. I intend my words to be an angel's nudge, encouraging you to trust the wisdom of your own amazing body.

ACKNOWLEDGEMENTS

I give thanks to Peter de Liefde, my publisher at Sense who has the vision and will to put this kind of creative work into the world. Thank you Patricia Leavy for your encouragement and sending me on to Sense. Thanks to the whole team at Sense and particularly Jolanda Karada, the Production Coordinator. Thanks to Jami McCarthy for her thoughtful editing on my draft. Thank you Mary Blaze for the beautiful art work on the front cover. I am in deep gratitude to all my students over the last several decades who have gone on the journey with me to bring back embodied ways of knowing, writing and living into their lives, research and work. The way all of you keep shining is birdsong. I also want to thank my colleagues and friends over the years who have walked with me and collaborated in one form or another. You have allowed for a much wider tribe to bring creativity, the body and the arts into the academy and I'm eternally grateful. There are more than I can name, in particular, I give thanks for Barbara Bickel, Mary Blaze, Mary Beth Cancienne, Diane Conrad, Diana Denton, Gene Diaz, Lynn Fels, Susan Gerofsky, Erica Grimm, Vicki Kelly, Carl Leggo, Rebecca Lloyd, Rebecca Lux Parks, Indrani Margolin, Susan McCaslin, Jodi Proznick, Kathryn Ricketts, Jim Sanders, Stephen Smith, and Sean Wiebe. You have sustained me more than you know. I thank my wider Interplay community and my Seattle Interplay group who have opened the way for many body stories told over the years. Big gratitude to Kaija Pepper for our ongoing meetings to encourage one another in our writing projects. For my beloved three sons – Lucas, Caleb, and Micah who have always been my teachers to live a passionate life and my greatest gift and joy. You three continue to be my inspiration and have my full heart. Enormous gratitude to my husband, Shawn, who abides with me in the deepest support and love, more than I could have ever asked or imagined.

The pieces listed below have appeared, some in altered form in the following journals and books:

Chapter 1, "Let the body out," Let the body out: A love letter to the academy from the body. In E. Malewski & N. Jaramillo (Eds.). *Epistemologies of ignorance in education.* Charlotte, NC: Information Age Publishing (2011), pp. 187–198. "Ancient yearning," and "What you say yes to" in *Wild tourist: Instructions to a divine tourist from the divine feminine.* New Westminster,

ACKNOWLEDGEMENTS

BC: Silver Bow Publishing (2016), pp. 52, 62. "Moist manna," "A curriculum of beauty." *Teacher Educational Quarterly*, (2002), 29(4), 119–123. "Crowdance" and "The great love story" in *Royal City Poets 5 Anthology* 2015. New Westminster, BC: Silver Bow Publishing (2015), pp. 82–84. "In praise of the kitchen studio" in *Blue skies* (2008).

We do not have bodies;
we are bodies.

We came from the belly and hips
and we must return there.

Snowber, *Dance as a Way of Knowing* (2012a, p. 55)

LET THE BODY OUT

live in your nature
eagle is not a salmon
show up for your life

I commend you, for giving me your attention. You have analyzed and grasped the concept of the body politic and the connections between the body, knowledge and power. You have researched the cultural reasons the body has been absent and present, revered and misused. Now I find myself party to a wide variety of discourses, taking place across many fields and disciplines. I am a hot subject and object; researchers are now taking me seriously. I am even being discussed at the desks of some of the finest institutions around the world.

This is a big feat. Yet in this presence there are absences. These absences are conspicuous and have implications for the intellectuals, scholars, artists, practitioners, and educators who speak about and live from the body. So now it is time for me to speak. I speak to you with a tender heart, and from all that I, the body, want you to live through mystery, paradox, and ecstasy. I am not a text and cannot be distanced like words read on a page. Words don't sweat or weep, moan or bleed. I do. I have come to remind and rebody you to remember a few ways to bring me back to the centre of your attention. I am more interested in being a centrefold than a fold.

I am a gift for you. Think of me as a personal navigation system to deeply listen to me and hear the possibilities of what can unfold within you, including pain and beauty. I am the all-inclusive map you have been yearning for, a free GPS system to your innermost longing. I am not found in one neat package. I am filled with the wonder and the limitations of all that it means to be an alive human being. It is through me that you feel the wind in your hair, the water on your skin and the sway in your limbs. I live through a sensuous knowledge. I am all about those many kinds of intelligences you speak of, that have been well theorized. I am the lifeblood of inspiration; it is I who puts breath into these intelligences. I am found not only in kinaesthetic or visual intelligence, but how you viscerally feel the waves of movement within your flesh, the flutter in your chest, the sigh in your voice, the release in your shoulders, the way you walk into your class or how you glance at a loved one.

I reside in the subtle sensations constantly flowing through you. I am your trusted inner voice. I am the feast for your eyes, the tactile knowing for your skin, and the smell of your sweat. I speak in a language that defies categories. It is the language of the flesh, ripe with carnal ways, which are often absent from the halls of the academy, institutions, and the boardrooms of corporations.

In a predictable fashion, I am known to be unpredictable. My sentences are formed with the grammar of the gut. This is a grammar that is often left at the doors when policies are being made or enacted. Though this is perhaps where I am most needed. What would it mean for decisions to be lead by the pulse of the body during an important merger or integrating a huge change to a higher-educational institution? How could attention to the body positively affect decision-making or attend to inclusiveness? You see, it has become in vogue to speak of intuition and imagination in many fields, including leadership, management, health, law, research, and teaching. The diverse fields within education, arts, counselling, and philosophy after all have had major thinkers and scholars that have cultivated other ways of knowing, although I'm always a bit of a side dish. The truth is sometimes the side dish, is the main dish, the ones you adore, like French fries!

AN ENFLESHED THEORY DANCES

There is a secret the body holds. How you access your imagination, intuition and perception lies within the body. Making a practice of listening to your imaginative, intuitive, and perceptive abilities activates the energy that lies dormant within your own pulsing body. You can know all the steps to a dance – a *plié*, a turn, a rhythm, or hand gesture, but the steps are theorizing. To truly dance the steps, you need to breathe life into them, to activate the soul – the bodysoul. Go beyond the steps to a place where you can dance again as a child does. I'm after a theory with flesh on it; a theorizing through the flesh.

So many of you let the rhythm of what delights you take second place, or worse, give it up completely. If you attended to the body as you do to the computer, we could really have a party, if not tea! I love to be moved, walked, spun, stretched, and expanded. I need breath and movement for living. I am often stopped from yawning. How I long to yawn in your seemingly endless meetings! Every profession or field has infinite meetings.

Why don't you take a break and let me stretch in the middle of your committee or departmental meetings? What if I could stretch, sigh, or even sit on the ground? I am scrunched for hours in front of a laptop. The fingers are getting a work out, but a huge part of me has been left behind. My goodness, it's as if you don't have hips or legs or pelvises for that matter. What about entertaining a pelvic inquiry? You have relegated the pelvis to live in the third world as if it is the forgotten sister. Bring her back! From the pelvis you were born and it is to the pelvis you must return to. Activate those hips dear and you may feel the sway of your own heart! A knowing that lies in the centre of your belly may reveal itself. A hidden voice may speak.

You of course, like everyone else, learned to "pay attention" by being still. This is not a true attention or a contemplative or alive stillness, but more like being frozen or immobilized, which of course results in stiffness. Contemplative stillness knows the rhythm of the breath and is in close contact with the heart. This is the sort of bodily attention where one recovers awe at each day.

It is time to make space for me as you did when you were a child. Abandon yourself once again to skipping rope and leaping frogs. Make noises and invent stories as often as brushing your teeth. Here is the place for astonishment and inspiration.

Some of you had begun your early career as professors in education as teachers, for you loved the child within yourself and the child without. Or you began your career as artists or actors because you loved to create as a child or as scientists because you loved to experiment. I am asking you to attend again as a child, the child who knows the body does not lie, but is the place where truth lives, however you may define that. Let me arise from the sitting postures I am in all day. Let me come out and play! Take your students through the physicality of the earth, transgress the boundaries of your confined spaces. The real act of transgression is to bring me to your class, let me out, find the body pedagogy of teaching. Here all teaching is a bodily act as well as mentoring students or colleagues for that matter. Or bring me to the health institution and hear your patients through the stories within their bodies. Let your body be brought to the listening process, where one listens with all of his or her being. You can't afford not to bring me.

And most of all remember this: it is time to play again. Instead of just hashing issues out with colleagues, go together to the woods, open up your sternums to the sky, smell the fragrance of the earth and be silent together. It is in the silences that the body has insight waiting to impart. If you allow the body with its senses into research, data collection, analysis and reflection, there may be a different world, a new "academy" – an academy of flesh available to you. You are called to survive and to thrive. Engage with all your physicality and return to nourishing body, soul, heart and intellect.

After all this life is about connection. Your body seeks to connect you to the magic of the life force through the magic of the body. You may all call it something different, but this is about living with *jouissance*, living with vitality and being deeply alive. Sip the body's glory in joyful times and may that deepen your endurance in the hard times. The body is not perfect, neither is your nose, back or hormones. Every human being lives with limits. Some more than others. Even the broken body takes its place in our lives. There are times when you are called to pause and pace. Slow down. Soothe oneself into the beauty of writing by hand, walking in shadow, eating mangoes and using more garlic. You are both researchers and searchers. Our lives are a place of research – a living search. It is all too easy to forget to search for and befriend the body.

Contained in this search and research is the rootedness to your humanness, your human beingness. You are often better at human *doing* than human *being*. Connection to your body is most alive in the spaces of being, the ontological space of being present – a bodily presence. So ask yourself, and right now: What does your body know? What does your body remember?

In what your body longs for lies the wisdom and the space for rejuvenation. Find the landscape for your expressions as you did when turning your torso in your mother's womb. I am no longer satisfied to be in the pockets of lives, institutions, academies or organizations. I want to be part of the full clothing – animating your life from within. Come back to what I have given you in the beginning.

Speak tenderly to me and let the wild/erness return or perhaps emerge for the first time. Let your own tissues and cells surprise you into its great mystery.

WHAT HAPPENED TO BODY KNOWLEDGE?

How did our intimate connection to the body get lost in the first place? How has our connection to the knowledge stored in our bodies become dormant? How did it come to be that knowledge that you had in the beginning of your life has now become inaccessible to you? There is so much knowledge, epistemologies and ontologies of all kinds. Yet, there are continual splits between theorizing and practicing, knowing and acting, listening and responding. Scholarly discourse has given attention to "the absent body," to the places where the body has not been heard, seen or felt. Having and living in a body is a birthright of being human, but the deeper truth is that you were all born with the knowledge that you *are* bodies, not just *have* bodies. This birthright contains a knowledge that is visceral, tactile, visual, audible and kinaesthetic. As your first love, you moved in your mother's womb and took delight in world outside with all your senses. Unfortunately, you soon learned from your culture and teachers that bodily knowledge was not valued as much as head knowledge. Excelling in the joy of swinging, playing in the mud, pounding on your pillow or listening to your belly doesn't typically earn you kudos or respect. In contrast, you likely would be praised for executing certain skill sets, such as those related to sports, or having to sit attentively in the classroom. But of course you soon found as you were schooled both within the culture, and institutions that this bodily knowledge was not high on the list of what was valued. A major mistake of schooling is the one that equates paying attention with sitting still. Sitting still creates a frozenness in the body, overriding the body's natural fluidity. The mind and body are so connected, that in fact, the mind ceases productivity in response to the body being cramped. When there's no room to breathe, the mind can become narrow. Of course everyone is getting this brain/body connection now, there is scientific proof after all.

What happens at an early age, happens without being conscious of it. Boys and girls grow into men and women who make agreements with themselves, about everything in life really, especially those things concerning their bodies. You learn at an early age, what is important to culture and societies is the appearance of the body. There is a focus on the external, rather than the internal body. This focus on the external body is what leads many of us to make consciously or subconsciously an agreement to not pay attention to the sensing, pulsing, breathing body. One of the reasons this happens is because for many it is easier to attend to what one looks like – a bad hair day, too-tight jeans or a roll in the belly.

More challenging is to be attentive to what is going on inside the body – the quality of your breath, whether there's tightness or ease or your postural alignment. Often when the mind takes over, multiple splits set in causing a disconnect from the body and many aspects of life. One of the most significant disconnects is to minimize the body as a wise source and experience of information. As you know, information can be received from the mind and from the body, but even more they are utterly connected. The impact of information from the gut leads to knowledge that won't soon be forgotten. For instance, the scent of a crab apple or cedar tree may uncover your entire childhood; the scent of rhubarb pie baking has multiple stories to tell. The memory of knowledge lies in your senses.

A loved one can tell you that h/she loves you over and over again, but unless you truly feel this with your heart, it can only be words. Or the reverse can happen, and one cannot mention the word love, but you feel this affection deeply. As humans you were designed to comprehend knowledge with your whole beings – mind, hearts, soul, imagination, flesh. Not all knowledge is the same, content being vastly different. But knowledge that is predominantly received in the mind can be dismissed, but once you get knowledge in the gut it is difficult to forget its impact. The nuances of knowing live in the places between your shoulders and loins, fingers and chest.

In some cultures and societies the mind and thought have been lauded over the body and feeling. All knowledge is useful, but until it reaches to the bones and drops into the cells you tend not to "get" it. An example, consider instructions for how to ride a bike. I could tell you how to move your arms and legs, how to connect your breath to their movements, etc., but until you engage in the visceral practice of riding a bicycle and your muscles develop the motor skills and memory, riding a bicycle will be a theory. Knowledge to and from the body comes via practice. Knowledge likes to get under the skin to have long lasting effects. A tactile knowledge, one where the grammar of the gut has its way.

REMEMBERING YOUR FIRST LOVE

What you know you still know. It just needs to be re/membered, re/bodied back to being. That is why I am writing you a love letter. Actually this whole book is a love letter, but in this chapter I lay the foundation. I am your first love, and I'm beckoning for you to return to me. Come with me and I will again teach you to listen to the churning in your stomach, the flutter in your chest, the loosening of your hips, the subtle sensations in your body, waiting to be discovered and uncovered. I am patient, but sometimes when I need to get your attention I break down. If you ignore me for a while, I grow louder until I get your attention. You think your deadlines are more important. Well your deadlines are not lifelines. I am your *lifeline*. I wait for you to come home and find the joy of being alive. I am a built-in spiritual director, able to guide you through the terrain in your life. It is all about noticing, a day-by-day listening. Make some time for me. Walk in the fresh air, even if it is raining. Stretch in the middle of a meeting. Have your tears and your laughter too. Luxuriate in the way paying attention to me can comfort you. This letter is about how to listen to me. This invites you home to yourself. It's an initiation to embodied knowledge.

Maybe you have made an unconscious contract to not listen to your own body. Maybe you feel that is necessary because of time pressure or other circumstances. For example, it could be that you assume the responsibility to answer all your emails within 24 hours or 12 or 3 hours, even if your body is exhausted and needs to rest. It's important to develop a daily practice that allows you to question what is best for your body. You have lots of years to work it out, so relax into a daily bodily practice of self-care. Don't see this as one more thing to accomplish. Remember your body is calling you back as a lover. Sometimes lovers forget about time and just relish in the beauty of the moment.

Make a contract with yourself that honours your body. Begin small; tiny, incremental steps are best. As you read through this book, breathe or sigh and take breaks to shake out your body. Then, return. This is a practice you could do with all your reading and writing. If you find you're getting distracted, stretch and expand, or take a walk. Return over and over again to your living pulse so you may once again be at home in your own skin. Connect to your longings. Accept and honour your limits. Let them be your teachers. Most of all, celebrate your quirks, for only you have them. That is the beauty. Celebrate that you are always called once again to your first love, the body you have and are.

And then, most importantly; what about your voice, your dear deep voice which articulates concerns in your personal and professional life? We spend half our lives finding our "voice" and then we are asked to put it into an articulation of knowledge that is privileged over many other kinds of knowledge. And one wonders sometime where is your *body* in your voice, both orally and in your literacy? How does your personal and professional voice interconnect? How can you honour your body's knowing in the midst of all the hats you wear? The body doesn't respond to or fit into formulas. Formulas or formulaic writing diminish the body's ability to come to language. All language comes out of the breath and tongue, the rhythms of language are visceral. And this is being caught on, in a few circles, but there is a long way to go to recognize and remember the body back to language. This would be a good travel plan: bring the body home to language. An all-inclusive excursion where the body infiltrates the way we write, speak, and even think.

You have been trained how to read and write. I am calling you back to a place where blood turns to ink, and flesh seeps into your words so they sing and pulse off the page, dancing into your readers' hearts and minds in a way that is truly re/membered. A kind of knowing that breathes vitality.

Race, culture, class, and gender undoubtedly form our perceptions and ways of being in the world. I have been left out of the conversation, unable to articulate body-based knowledge. The knowledges' of race, culture, class, and gender are typically expressed in mediums where procedural, rational and logical thought are privileged over artistic, intuitive, and visceral thought. Slowly, this is really changing, I am still concerned about how your voice disappears through these discourses. For some of you, it might work, but I would suggest that many of you are longing or beginning to desire a more organic articulation of your voice. When your true voice comes out, all you have to do is just *show up for your life.*

The best you can bring to both words and worlds is yourself, because no one can be like you. The world needs all of you, hundreds of thousands of different ways you perceive, live, think, in your different fields. The world needs embodied voices, ones that not only have astute things to say or write, but be expressed in a way that reduces the distance often contained in sharing knowledge. The world needs a knowledge that is intimate, one that throbs with humanity. Only when the body returns to its language can there be the kind of fullness that is possible. The return is an act of transgression. It is an act of emancipation, creating body-wise people.

Return to your voice in all its beauty and depth. Authentic speaking and hearing can occur between yourself and others when the mind, heart, soul, and body are given free reign in the voice. You might be asking, "how do I do this?" To do this, is a small day-to-day practice honouring the body. As you make room for me, you will be surprised how I pop up in your sighs and words.

What I yearn for is to find the origin of words, which have breath in them. These are words dropping from within and without, words that dance on your skin. There are many things you know, and many things you don't know. The knowledge that is hidden, obscured, and waiting to be grown in your hearts and in your minds is a knowledge that is absent, but in its absence is strength. The absence is waiting. The wisdom is waiting. In our attention to letting the body have its way, letting the body be part of all we say, do, and write, a new kind of knowledge is born. This is what artists know. This is what athletes know in the flow of their movement. This is what scientists know on the edge of discovery. This is the heart of the creative. I want academics, lawyers, musicians, ecologists, and scientists to be outrageously creative. Return to the play of language, surprise yourself. Drink deep of your own flesh, which calls forth a listening to all the rumblings of your life. I am in your midst, in the small acts of dailiness within and without you.

You've got the "footnoting" styles down. And you may notice that this book has few footnotes, as an intentional act of listening to rhythm. I am now asking for you to get your feet in your notes. Take notes with your feet. Teach on your feet. Practice artmaking with your feet. Practice therapy with your bellies. Let your soles become where your soul breathes. Take off those shoes, boots, high-heels and place your worn feet on the earth and let your feet tell you where to go, what to research, where to write the next sentences.

There is never enough of integrating the body into all the diverse ways of writing. The body does not want to be bracketed, or just be utilized as a semi-colon. The body wants to be a comma, constantly breaking up every little intention and action. The body wants to live in multiplicity and thrive in multiples. I am after ecstatic living, even within institutions, be they academic or corporate.

To let me out is to truly let me be. To let me be is to let the river flow rather than pushing the river. By now in your life, you may have managed to get yourself through several institutions, have several degrees and have had a variety of jobs and relationships. You are highly skilled, attuned to the nuances of your field and have a wealth of knowledge and experience. You might have a stack of books by your bed, dozens of emails to answer, and have an over-booked schedule for the next few months. In this case, as in all, you really can't afford to live without the wisdom of the body. I will be the one who will bring you balance, rhythm and health. Chances are if you don't listen to me, I also may be the place where much of your physical or emotional pain is located. So, I really need to be let out to play.

Letting me out is like building your immune system. So dangle your feet. Skip on the beach, lay in the grass and watch clouds. This too is research. I think of lying in the grass as a horizontal inquiry, one that connects your body to the earth. The earth loves to hold you. Here, as one form shifts into another, your body-spirit can imagine life's possibilities.

From all this talk of the body, you may be wondering where the practices of keeping the body fit figure into the equation. I am concerned with your physical sustainability as I am that you come alive to yourself, others, and the world through your senses. I want you to return to a sensual knowing where you are rejuvenated in the eros of the everyday. What wisdom, knowledge and experience do your senses have to communicate to you? How does sound, colour, light, texture, touch and smell inform your moments? What does sensuous knowledge have to teach and how can you trust your senses as a place of wisdom?

The body is trustworthy. It will break down and change from injury or age; you can trust this will happen. You can also trust there is a wellspring of wisdom residing in your cells. This inner guide is waiting for you to consult with it. Speak tenderly to your body, speak to your body as a lover, luxuriate in the seasons of who you are becoming. Even your limits are a source of information and grace.

It must be mentioned that the body is a place of paradox. None of you are left untouched by pain, suffering or loss. Here is the place I have often called, "paradoxology" – in praise of paradox. You are invited into deep vulnerability and it is in this place that worlds can open up to you. Now it is not as if you have to suffer to have meaning, but your fragility as a human is something you share. It has its specific colour in your life and can be a place of beauty and transformation.

Take for example a dancer who has a severe injury and must learn to find other sources of movement to express the inner resonances. An injury or limit can invite one into moving in ways and combining other forms as voice, poetry, or site-specific work that may not otherwise occurred. The limits in the body can be a place for grace, an opening to the unexpected. No matter what, the body does age, you can count on this reality. The body needs to continually reinvent ways of moving and living that express and sustain vitality.

You may not be able to run anymore because of your bad knees, but what about kayaking? You may not be able to play hockey, but what about yoga? If you are in discomfort try a massage. There are many ways and alternatives to stay connected to and move your body. Through limits and constraints, you are challenged to leave predictable ways of moving and change the repertoire. This requires you to be an embodied creative. Comfort zones can be left behind, opening us up and discovery is a never-ending source of delight.

For example, you may be called to change the speed in which you undertake your days. Slowing down could be an act of transgression. When the body slows, it gives you a chance to really feel your feet rooted on the earth, to experience a sense of being grounded. When you feel your roots, you can fly. Levity and gravity are partners.

The body roots you inward and connects you to the interior life and what deeply matters. You may not even know what that is, but your deepest longings are waiting to be uncovered. You need all your strengths, including the physical, emotional, intellectual and spiritual for the journey of your life. Two lovers' strength and health resides in both their solitude and companionship. The body needs time alone and together with others. And as lovers need to rediscover the beauty in shared presences, delighting in small and often simple things, so too the body needs to find these small delights. The smell of the sea or pine, an expanse of the chest, releasing to wet tears, or a spontaneous burst of joy.

Rediscover your own dear body-guide, foot by foot, hip by hip, heart by heart. I have been longing for you to come home for quite some time now, and it really is about living more effortlessly with more ease and more delight. Bodily knowing and understanding is your life guide. It is always with you as you search and research. Now go let your body stand up and stretch.

BODYPSALM FOR REMEMBERING BACK THE BODY

Remember back the body
flames in the belly
calling one to live
as each day is the first and the last
Your life is a precious
entity of cells and blood
quirks and sentences of glory

Remember back the passion
don't let the awe
slip from your fingers
toes, hips, pelvis and voice
Draw back into presence your own calling
for what you are meant to do and be
on this glorious planet
coupled with the paradox of terror and beauty

It is not only the earth
which needs greening
but your own precious soul
sometimes lost in the meetings, emails or laundry

Remember back all of you
messy and unpredictable
veins pulsing with a hopefulness
to thirst for more.
Hunger is your spiritual director
Coming in all forms –
Discontent or agitation
Press on to what is nudging you
breathing you back into
inhabiting your own body

The calling of your life
lies at the door
waiting for you.

In solitude, ideas are nurtured into an incarnational reality
where art is eventually birthed, syllable by syllable,
movement by movement, pigment layered upon pigment.
Solitude teaches one the art of attentiveness
to the opening of a bud, to a child's startling questions,
and to the beat of one's own heart.

Snowber, *Writing from the Body.* (1995, p. 3)

SOLITUDE AND PHYSICALITY

solitude beckons
dwell in your own company
coming home to heart

Solitude beckons our bodies to come into a love relationship with ourselves. From our elbows to our bellies, the inside to the outside we are invited into living more deeply into the paradox of what it means to be full human beings. Solitude can often be thought of as time alone or away, and emphasis is on the aloneness of this set apart time. I am interested in the quality of solitude, a kind of gourmet place to be rejuvenated and rediscover what is at the heart of our lives. Solitude is also often associated with the mind or mindfulness, yet the mind is intertwined with the body, and my question continues to be what happens when there are practices in our lives, which foster a connection between physicality and spirituality or cognition and intuition or the fingers and pulse? Here there is a bodily mindfulness. Mindfulness connected to being full-bodied and fully inhabiting the body. Perhaps one could call it *bodyfullness*.

There was a time, when the word "scholar" had the connotation of a life marked by a time to reflect and nourish the life of the mind. But the life of the mind is never separate from the body. It is often when one enters a kind of flow where there is an integration of mind, heart and body that one has a deep receptivity to what comes. Artists and athletes, musicians and mediators, dancers and inventors or children playing all know these moments where time stops, and brilliance happens. A physiological rhythm occurs where a kind of surrender happens, where body and mind, heart and soul are in unison. There is scientific language which explains these places, and neuroscience has dedicated volumes to the logistics, but for the purposes of this book, I invite you to consider what it would mean to have a practice where physicality and mindfulness meet.

I have never had the luxury for huge amounts of solitude as an adult, particularly in the last few decades as a single parent raising amazing sons and holding a tenure-track faculty position as well as attending to the complexities of a full life. However, this is the case for many as we live multi-coloured and multi-tasked lives, where we are continually being encouraged to be good human "doings" rather than human "beings." As leaders, teachers, citizens, artists, musicians, carpenters, lawyers or health practitioners emphasis is continually on how much one does or performs. Seldom is there emphasis on being. Professional development in all sectors of employment is important, and rarely does one get reimbursed to go on a meditation or spiritual retreat or kayak trip to enhance your professional life, and yet perhaps this is exactly what is needed.

HORIZONTAL INQUIRY AND SABBATH

I have often thought that teachers don't need one more workshop to aid them in their pedagogy or curriculum development, but really need a rest. And rest is not just a nap, although I am a firm believer in naps, and I have developed an inquiry around being horizontal. Horizontal inquiry is what I call it, and I actually do take my students outside and tell them to look at the sky for five minutes and write about their experience. We have often forgotten how to dream and waste time. And yet it is often in wasting time where the muse is found and kindled. As Thomas Merton has said many years ago, "Hurry ruins saints as well as artists" (1961, pp. 98–99).

The rest that I am speaking of is not just a physical rest, but one where deep replenishment is at the heart of a reprieve. In the fast-paced life that we live in the twenty-first century, seldom is there time for a reprieve in the midst of dailiness. And if there is, there are usually earphones attached to our ears. I would like to resurrect the meaning of the word Sabbath and its connection to the body. Sabbath, being a place that is set apart, a place where the ordinary becomes sacred.

I find Sabbath when I swim, particularly at the lake. Sabbath shifts my relationship to time, or said so poignantly by Jewish theologian Abraham Heschel, "Sabbath celebrates time rather than space…to turn from the results of creation to the mystery of creation" (1951/2005, p. xviii). I lay on my back doing the back-stroke gazing at the changing clouds in the sky. Cedar and green immerse my sight, and dragonflies sometimes swarm in the air. If I am particularly lucky, an eagle will fly ahead and I go into astonishment. Here is horizontal inquiry for me, where on my back, my neck is supported, and limbs move to the rhythm of my breath. I am catapulted into immense gratitude for being alive. I am revitalized and can begin again.

Calling our bodies back to themselves is timely on the planet. An alternative rhythm is established and one hearkens to another kind of time. It is a place to have compassion on our limits and know we are not perfect, but are perfect in our imperfection. Vulnerability calls one to solitude, and here lies a great gift. The limits one often perceives is the invitation to slow down, participate in a slowdance, where savouring becomes a verb in our lives, or perhaps for the first time. One can also savour in groups, duets, trios or public spaces, but there is a special place for dwelling and lingering with ourselves and nourishing solitude as a practice. Often times it is only when one gets sick, is there permission to stay home, be quiet, and even in our limitations, a quiet can set in and pull one from the tyranny of details. Solitude waits patiently for us – even in small spurts to bring us to dwell into our bodyhearts.

I have often thought that it is the constant attention to details, woven into hundreds of emails a day, and meetings for hours, and coordinating multitude calendars of people, which rob me of the capacity to linger in the moment, which keeps calling me. The moment could be as simple as leaving my attention from the computer screen to watch the birds fly by my window, or listen to the tightness in my shoulder and leave my desk and dance for 5 minutes, and return refreshed. My body is a constant reminder to alert me to what is really important. My own sense of over-responsibility will delay what truly gives me life. I may need to shift responsibility to being responsive and respond to what I know deep inside.

After my children had grown and moved out, I moved from my family home into a condo. One of the aspects I loved about where we had lived was the proximity to the forest – tall cedars and creeks, eagles flying ahead even in the suburbs outside Vancouver in British Columbia. The paths surrounded us as we lived on the edge of a small mountain. Now, I live close to the Fraser River, overlooking a city, and I am learning the teachings of this remarkable working river. But I have missed the trails in my backyard, where wood and words would meet me in my daily walks. I have seen in the distance trees from my window in my condo and patio, and sometimes hear coyotes at night. I just have never been able to fathom where these coyotes would live. Assuming the trees did not hold any paths, since they weren't as large in scope of my previous domain, I did not venture near this particular geography.

Recently I walked to the beginning of this land, and went down steep stairs, and realized to my wild delight, there was a beautiful path covered with huge, yellow, wet leaves offering their beauty to the ground, and enveloped in a variety of plants, trees and species, which were indigenous to the area.

Close to my home, a world was waiting for my attention. Solitude is close to home, waiting. It always asks and gives more than I can ask or imagine, waiting as the path out my door, till I was ready to arrive. And here I found more than I could have dreamed as I took each step into a kind of time, which nourished my inner and outer self.

Over the years, I have often thought that what I most need is *to cooperate with my own nature*. However, it is easy for me to lose the essence of my own nature, with professional and family demands coming from all angles. There is a vivacious, extroverted, gregarious self, but there is also the self, who is nourished in the darkness, the still places, or the fierce landscapes where wind, sea and salt sweep my being. A practice of solitude rooted in physicality allows me to keep greeting my deep nature.

I have never been fortunate enough to have mounds of time, or extra support to take hours and days of solitude. But even 10 to 30 minutes of this kind of time, allows for opportunities for revitalization. And from this reinvigoration, what really could be the effects? On my creating or writing, researching, teaching or performing, living or parenting, loving and learning? These small practices surely are what creates a sustainable life and open us to new ways of being and perceiving. Never underestimate small moments which become lifelines.

EMBODIED PRACTICES

I am proposing not just time to be alone, but the way in which one *inhabits* time. The body can be the entrance to inhabiting time, which is expansive and generative. I have lived this out in my own life for decades and I now look back and see the relationship between productivity and small embodied practices. My morning practice of walking and writing in small portions has been a foundational grounding. My walking became my writing, my writing became my walking, and I could not distinguish from walking, listening, praying, being, writing, or dancing. All was a place to listen to the wells of inspiration. My brain, overcrowded with details, could slowly rest for a few minutes, or half-hour and I could give my limbs to the words and wonders which would come through me. *Inspiritus*. Breath to body. Body to earth. Body to breath. I began to incorporate this into all my classes I teach – undergraduate, graduate and pre-service education for teachers. These comprise Graduate classes on Embodiment and Curriculum Inquiry or Doctoral classes in Arts-Based Research or Undergraduate classes in Movement Education. I invite students to begin a practice of solitude which connects to physicality; walking or running, kayaking or writing, but there has to be a designated time of 15–20 minutes, and may need to leave their housemates or family for this time. I ask them to write out of these experiences. It is amazing that when someone has to do something as a requirement what happens. We give ourselves permission to give our bodysouls what we wanted all along. More astounding ideas, epiphanies, insights, and beginnings for theses and dissertations came out of these times than anything else. Ideas are massaged and nurtured into a physical reality when steeped in the tea of solitude.

Creativity is birthed syllable by syllable, step by step as one opens to the attentiveness to the beat of one's own breath and heart. The art of listening is being rehearsed. A rehearsal for the brilliance of one's own beautiful life. Embodied practices are the entry point for inhabiting one's own extraordinary life and become as important as rules of grammar. This is the grammar of the heart, the grammar of the gut, taking action into form.

I bring my classes through a walk in silence, so the senses are more fully alert and alive to the shades and colours of the natural world and sounds humming in the universe. Most folk are not used to walking in silence with others, and it can be uncomfortable at first, but it can also be a slow descent into a communion with oneself in community. There is something deeply profound to experience silence in a concert of other humans. The pressures finally release to speak or engage in a conversation and eventually there is a sweet intimacy of experiencing the natural world in an aria of silence, where creation is singing and we are guests on this planet experiencing the wonder and invitation to be present to what is within us. More times the kind of writing and conversations that came out of just a half hour of walking in silence has brought an encyclopedia of insights.

We are invited here to see the macro in the micro or the micro in the macro, which is at the centre of paying attention. Solitude and silence strip away the urgency of time, and one is invited into what is infinite; to experience *kairos* time or unmeasured time, and leave *chronos* time or chronological time. In *chronos* time moments are measured, but in *kairos* time one can be swept into the eternal present and infinite possibilities are born.

What if the world could have a radical shift in the workplace by honouring professional development as places of solitude, rejuvenation, and embodied practices? I have often thought it would be wonderful if I could have my faculty be a place of wellness, instead of overwork, exhaustion, and toxicity; a place where we are reenergized.

What if we saw the connection between embodied practices and research, artmaking, or making policy? I am really after inspiration, and one needs to be inspired whether you are a scientist or artist. Often the reason we don't take the time needed for practices, which regenerate, is because we are under the myth that we are losing time. But what if it was the opposite, and by engaging, our time became richer and fuller; so vibrant it was more effective? What if we all went out and took a walk together for fifteen minutes? How could simple embodied acts change the world and ways of being?

This book is not a new fancy methodology, but an invocation to bring aspects to our lives which will infuse our vocation, creativity, research, skills that can bring restoration and inspiration. A true breath-letting into the life that we are called to live. To truly cooperate with our own nature. Solitude beckons to return to the delicious place of living in gratitude and what might have been ordinary transforms into what is extraordinary. These simple acts of connecting our embodied lives in a rhythm of solitude can bring us to our hearts' home. And in this place everything is sacred.

BODYPSALM FOR SOLITUDE

Sip the sweetness
of your own solitude
a communion with yourself
in the season given to you

a mist sings over your limbs
softening your joints
releasing fluid between your bones
here is the oil to tenderize
demands and responsibilities

what some may perceive
as loneliness is the invitation
for a rare union –

the fragrance of silence
bringing space in the spine
undergirding each turning
in the fall of your life
revealing heart's yearning

Be embraced
through a l o n e n e s s
the door to the inside
and secret passage
to the Beloved
and entrance to the home
of being loved
& being love

Retreat
in the nest
of your inner habitat
and find your deep nature
greeting you.

The body has a pronouncement all to itself,
which is felt in the lived experience of fingers and toes,
shoulders and hips, through the heart of veins
and on the breath of limbs.

Snowber, *Dancing on the breath of limbs: Embodied inquiry as a place of opening.* (2014a, p. 119)

WAKING UP TO THE SENSUOUS

torso sighs wonder
joints stretched to broken sky
thick with shimmering

Waves break, cedars reach to sky, breath expands and life's energy pulses through the body. The language of the earth and the language of the body are deeply connected. From the sternum to the hips resides a place of awakeness and what is called sensuality or sexuality is so much more. Embodied ways of inquiry are an invitation to dwell more richly in the territory of the sensual life, where all of life is both sensual and sacred. Sensuality is a way of being; how one engages with themselves, and the way one lives and perceives and responds in the world. Our sensuality is a birthright connected to what it means to be human. Feeling the wind on the face, the blood of life running through our cells, the ecstasy of a bending tree, the freshness of water on flesh, the colour of an apricot, or the joy of jumping are all forms of sensuous knowing.

LANDSCAPE OF OUR BODIES

When we tap into the love of creation, the power of water running down the mountains, and the sensuous language of the colours in the landscape, we are connected to the landscape of our bodies. The natural world is humming with the sounds and sights of eros, just as immersion in our daily lives can be an opera of unfolding beauty. As human beings on this planet we are beckoned to live in the world with the fullness of our bodies, which uncovers gestures and sounds, feelings and caresses, sights and smells in the textures of each day. And in this place our bodysouls are vibrating.

Often as children, if we are fortunate, we have the experience of abandoning the body while running on the beach, gliding arms through the wind, or playing in the mud. I have many of these recollections. I was fortunate to be brought up in an island town where the elements of ocean and wind were my playmates. During summer rains I would run down the street in my bathing suit, letting the warm rain soak me or dig for clams in the blackened mud. I recall the magic of snow days and the delight of my own children surrendering to weather.

Snow days seldom happen in the Pacific Northwest, where I raised my children, and when snow did come to baptize the earth we were invited into what I would call snow sensuality – days marked by the constant interaction of play and snow. My boys and I each found our ways of abandoning our bodies to the snow and feel the invigoration of weather through our fingertips. One child ran into the snow and made a snow angel. Another lay in snow with his mouth open wide catching the luminosity of flakes. I walked for hours and let dusk unwrap me in the changing colour reflected off white and green cedar. The following poem emerged from the joy of watching one child surrender to a winter day.

Moist Manna

You lay prostrate
snow bound
to ground
under canopy
of virgin flakes
mouth wide-open
catching moist manna

Ten-year old son
having snowday
you should be at school
but I let you stay home
taking in a curriculum
of slowed time
noticing white beauty
caressing shades of green
cedars open branches
a prayer of surrender

Could there be
an aesthetics of first
fallen snow

in a geography
where rain
is the main meal?

I revel in watching
you watch
snow fall
you abandon
full body and mind
to snow's rhythm
you invite me
to lay down and watch
you tell me of
family of birds
you saw fly above.

When I called
the school, to tell them
you'd be home
they asked if you were
sick
I said –
you were under the weather
but I meant
literally
you needed to lie
beneath the weather
learn its texture
first-hand
body-absorbed
perception through
touch, taste, smell.
You invited yourself
into a body aesthetic.

I wonder why
as adults, we forget
to lie down

in the textures of
the natural world
and behold the
beauty of what
falls in our arms.

At what time in our growth did we start limiting ourselves in abandoning our bodies to nature? Why is it sanctioned for the children to immerse with their whole beings, but for adults it is frowned upon to delight in a full body experience? Let's make snow angels and dance freely on the beach.

I question if we are really missing something on this earth, when our bodily experience becomes dictated by cultural norms rather than a turning and tuning to the impulses within which connect us to waves and weather. Sure, we are "allowed" abandonment in the throes of intimacy or a hockey game. There is a way of being intimate with the world and ourselves that allows for a fuller body engagement with meaning. A way that could be deeply satisfying, even breathtaking.

SENSUAL ART OF LIVING AND BEING

Our sensuality and sexuality can include a wider engagement of living as a sensual act – a sensual art. *This is the sensual art of living and being.* Here is a spiritual practice embedded in a physicality, which can be the foundation for our physicality. This can be expressed with another or alone. There are no clear steps or curricula that lead one on a linear path. One fumbles into the pain and sometimes fumbles into the wonder. It is an improvisation in unforeseen territory. You must encounter the unknown to be known, the unforeseen to be seen. Love in the big sense of the word gives us the fuel to take the next step; growing into, growing down into the love of self.

The animating force of life is called by many names: eros, desire, love, life-force, God/dess, spirit, or soul. Whatever it is called, it truly is what connects us to ourselves, our interior world, to others, and to all creation. All of creation is connected through love – from the love that gestated my sons in my womb to the love that makes our tulips grow, to the love which brings the birds' singing to our patio to the love which brings words to the page or paints to the canvas. This love in the territory of the heart cannot be taken away. There lies the fallacy that we can manufacture or produce it, or perpetuate it by another's love. Loves will come and go. Parents will be buried, children may get cancer, and lovers or partners may change. The love that runs in the streams of the universe and within our hearts, will endure. The beautiful words of the Indian poet Tagore (1997, p. 55) capture these connections.

The same stream of life that runs through my veins night and day runs through the world and dances in rhythmic measures.

I feel my limbs are made glorious by the touch of this world of life. And my pride is from the life-throb of ages dancing in my blood this moment.

Eros is the life force that runs through our veins; it's the energy that animates creation and creatures. It cannot be confined to the bedroom. Eros infuses life into all our interactions. It is a partnership between ourselves and creation, between one person and another, between colleagues, students, friends, lovers, and ultimately in relation to our own selves and our own creativity. Eros is the life force, which breathes and enlivens us to the life that wants to be lived in us. When we are vibrantly alive we know eros in our cells.

Eros fuels us for being lovers in the world. Not only lovers in a romantic relationship, but lovers of people, lovers of the planet, lovers of the numinous, lovers of words, colours, gestures, art, animals, poetry and food.

LIVING ROMANTICALLY

The call to live romantically is upon us. To live romantically is not only for couples, partners, boyfriends, or girlfriends. It is for everyone to fall in love with all of life. Living romantically can be sensed in a slow turning of the light or in small beauties of the shape of a red pepper, or the colour of pomegranates. I know these may seem like privileged states, but even in the most difficult situations, there are morsels of beauty to be found, in the cherishing of a human life.

I was fortunate to be brought up by an artistic mother, who was steeped in the culture of the old ways of Armenia and integrated that to modern life. Every vegetable was a piece of art. This was even more pronounced after she returned from the grocery store and washed all the apples and eggplant, peppers and celery, oranges and parsley. She carefully stacked the multi-coloured vegetables in the dish drainer as if creating a modern sculpture to go on display at the Museum of Modern Art, which she was faithful to bring me to. The attention in placing sumptuous vegetables in an artful pile could have been a performance art piece! As a child, my attention was brought to the outrageous colour of cooking with eggplant and pepper, parsley and onions. It was as if each plant was contributing to a gourmet feast. Beneath the skin of plum black is what I now call eggplant, and many poems have come out of what I thought was uninteresting as a child. The small beauties of daily life still infuse my body and soul. I thankfully have passed that to my three sons. Here is one of those poems I wrote dedicated to my mother.

In praise of the kitchen-studio

she created beauty
in strife, aftermath
of genocide, she
escaped but the
heart does not cease
to know the lament
of the forefathers
and foremothers
of the old country

at eleven she made
paper roses, and
sold them in Cambridge, Mass
brought the reapings
to her family

at seventy-three, the year
before her death, she still
was bringing flowers to life
after my father died –
nothing could stop her
arranging living petals
into modern art

our kitchen was
transformed into an
art studio, either
cooking with colour
or creating colour

through sculptural
objects and plant life

I have kept the tradition
of my artist-mother
knocked out a wall
in my kitchen/dining area
and put a wooden floor in
it doubles as a dance
studio, torso ecstatic

kitchens are places
of love: creating food, art,
dance, exchange of hearts
through flesh
and always, always
there shall be flowers

there is strife too in kitchens –
tears and conflict
but connections usually
win out, the ripeness
of beauty over a life-time

we are made and
re-made in the
kitchen-studio
colours of soul
brought to brilliance
in ordinary living.

One must not only eat food, but also digest its colours, a food group all to themselves. My mother teaching me to pay attention to the sensual details of food, colour and light formed the curriculum of my childhood. That level of attention continues to be a staple of what I hold dear and integrate into my teaching. My students write odes to strawberries and peppers, stones and sea glass; unravelling the depths of each fruit and vegetable through the senses. Often my students think they cannot write a poem, and yet five minutes of sitting with a strawberry or tomato allows them to wake up their senses where the juice of the vegetable truly turns to ink!

There are stigmas one can have about the creative process, whether it is singing, writing, or acting. Self-doubt and insecurities can raise their alarming heads. One can be proficient in one creative form, but swear off another. We can think it is only the professional imaginators that can do the creating. However, we are all called to create, just as we are called to breathe. It is not optional, but rather what it means to be human. The process is available to all human beings. After all, one does not have to be a professional chef to relish in cooking a delicious meal. The same is true for the artistic process. I have seen and heard more beautiful poems come out of prompts for writing odes to vegetables, than giving any formula for a sonnet. The senses wake us up to the wonder of life and we roam in the halls of creativity.

LIVING EXOTICALLY

When we think of the sensual, some of us may dream of tropical places, laying on the beach, feeling the salted and sea air on our faces, the breeze in our hair and on our skin. I sometimes wonder if we spend more time dreaming of these spaces than actually nurturing them in our daily lives. After all, only the few can take the time or have the privilege of funds to afford weeks of delicious holidays. There are many, many ways to let the body relax into nature, whether that is hiking the mountains, lying on the beach, sailing the blue ocean, or riding a bike around the neighbourhood. So how can we engage in this kind of wonder in the days we are balancing the demand of work schedules, deadlines, children, partners, lovers, aging parents, or whatever our responsibilities in life entail? We are often dictated by schedules, emails, correspondence of every shape and form. I invite you to practice interruptions, and find pockets of physical reprieve that have the potential to call you back to romancing your body back to care. And all our daily activities can be a place to celebrate, even cherish the gift of being sensual spiritual human beings.

To cherish our bodies as sacred is a spiritual act. The body and soul have the capacity and promise to be lovers never truly wanting to be apart, or thought of as separate. One is always thinking of the other. We are embodied human beings, not disembodied, even if not much encourages the act of embodiment. How much more sensuality can we find in another and in life? Bathing, folding laundry, gardening, doing dishes, giving and receiving massages, brushing hair, hugging and caressing – each of these acts create spaces for an embodied engagement with the world. Each of these gestures is connected to the place of sacred being.

If we dare to inhabit our bodies as sensuous spaces we experience the delicious quality of being alive sensually through our daily acts. It fascinates me that so many people take themselves on all-inclusive trips to find rest and access the exotic all the while the exotic is alive within them. The wild tourist is within us. I have a little book of poetry called, *Wild Tourist* (2016) and the theme is to live exotically.

Living exotically

There is a vast country waiting
within you to be discovered.
You don't even have to leave home
and there is a Fourth World country awaiting.
We speak of First and Third world and yet there is
still another world you have not visited.
Here no travel arrangements need to be made.

No airports, ferries or flight deals.
This is the supreme flight package;
flies directly to the delicious abyss within you
where true exoticism lies.
There are tastes, smells and sights
which are untold,
and only you can go on this trip.

There will be different species for each of you.
Be the explorer of your own inward travels.
Instead of just travelling to exotic places...

Live exotically.

IN PRAISE OF HIPS

Our perception of our bodies affects how we inhabit them. We think we have hips, not that we are hips. We act as if our pelvises were containers, not that we are pelvises. All the parts of our bodies can be a place of inquiry and wisdom. Perhaps it is time to listen to what our hips and pelvises have to say. To see the world through the hips' eye certainly would give a whole new meaning to the word hipsters.

I'm here to invite you to bring all the parts of our bodies to what it means to live and be present to ourselves and others. The hips have been marginalized and have wisdom waiting to be discovered. We can handle the hips for sex, but what about the pure enjoyment of walking. How many of you luxuriate in sauntering? What every happened to strolling? In fact as you are reading this, perhaps you should just go out for a stroll – slowing your steps down and taking in the world through all your senses.

We can't seem to celebrate curves, the juicy, lively place where light falls and shifts in the circles of flesh. I stand in praise of hips, in praise of the pelvis. Here one may find centre, the place that truly carries us, no doubt the place where we give birth, experience wonder of union. Hips are strong and big enough to sustain our torsos, round and curvy enough to welcome the stresses of life and delicious enough to be touched and caressed. What if we just lived more deeply into our pelvises? I invite my students to discover their hips, perhaps for the first time. This is pelvic inquiry! What is the ramification of a culture that has lost its centre, whose centre of the body is in the head or the throat. We are out of touch with the emotional, the intuitive, and the bold beauty of surprise. Let us call back the hips as a space of wonder. Let us inhabit the hips and pelvis as old friends, and let them guide us home. You don't need to go on an all-inclusive trip, you just need to come home to the body.

All can be an invitation into sensuous living. The *practice of living sensuously* in all of life is a practice towards deeply honouring our sexuality and creativity. The fecundity of our sexual lives can ebb and flow. Whether we're involved in a sexual partnership or not, each day, we can drink the juices of what life has to offer us. We can revel in the making of luscious meal. We can luxuriate in writing a variety of forms, as lovemaking. We are lovers in the world, called to engage with its ideas, words, colours and wonder. And here our words may emerge with a kind of aliveness we might never have thought possible.

BODYPSALM FOR CELEBRATING THE SENSUOUS

You are a juicy orange
papaya split in half
mango on fire
wrapped in the luxuriousness
of a wo/man with flesh and heart
tender and strong
waiting to be honoured
by your own deep soul.

It is the life-force
energy of life itself – eros of day
the pulsing blood of vibrancy
running through your cells
enlivening the fabric of your being
which is the ground of your sexuality.

Here is the template
to embrace your own temple
the widening one of love
living in your solar plexus
connected to the creation of the universe.

It is not the breasts, chests,
vagina, penis that holds your sexuality
but what rises within you
and works in harmony
with your dear body

You can so easily confuse the
outer as the source of beauty
and the entrance to sexual aliveness
when you are being awakened
from a much deeper centre
and your sensual knowledge
calls you home
to the delight of presence
the wind on your chest

the expanse in your back
the thrill of naked feet in sand
places of release
invite you to sense from the inside out

now is the time
to love back your body to itself
live in a state of open
where the cords of fire
will rip through your body
and you will know
the deep gift of your own vitality
feeding the heart of sexuality
where all of life is a bedroom
to be awake to each moment
loving each breath

in this place is an ancient shrine
located deep within your own crevices
calling you forth to your own juice
the desire is already within you
it only needs to be honoured
for its pure nature
it is what calls you to the divine
to yourself and to the other

and it is not your hips or pelvis
which is sexy, but how you let
the energy of life soar and dance
through your pelvis to say yes
to its own truth

here is your ground
here is your flight.

The body is the canvas for creativity.
We paint with our hands, dance with our feet,
sing with our breath, and sculpt with our palms.
Our very beings are creative—
we are made with the glorious impossible—
ears that hear, flesh that remembers,
pulse that regulates, and hair that protects.

Intuition resides in the sinews of the flesh
where tissue can be transformed to wonder.

Snowber, *Visceral Creativity: Organic Creativity in Teaching Arts/Dance Education.* (2013, p. 253)

WRITING FROM THE BODY

they wait like lovers
pages to write your musings
ink and blood are friends

Breath beckons to come into your words. Pulsing into a place where a rhythm of blood and bone can be transformed to ink. Though many think that writing is something for just the mind, it is also for the body. Language originates through orality, where words are formed in breath and saliva, tongue and throat and recesses of the belly. It wasn't long ago when there was a culture of storytelling, and TV, email, and Internet were not present; one had to rely on presence. Be present. Be with presence. Guests and families would go to the living room and tell stories; ones which might have been passed down for years, and animation and language was a true love affair.

I was fortunate to grow up in a family where meals were saturated with liveliness, stories and colourful laughter marinated in the tones of my father's crazy accents. He may have been politically incorrect in this day and age, but it was deeply embedded in my skin that everyone had a story of arriving from somewhere with the intricacies, difficulties and marvels of different cultures. After supper we would congregate in the living room with our guests. My mother would share the Hindu dancing she had studied for many years with the well-known dancer, La Meri, who was known as the "Queen of Ethnic Dances," bringing Indian and Spanish dance forms to the West. I am still haunted by the ease and grace of my mother's hands, arms and limbs flowing through the air. She lived up to her name Grace. I thought all families in the sixties in New England would naturally engage in dancing and storytelling. When I came to realize it was uncommon, I became increasingly grateful for my combination of the Armenian heritage of my mother and the Irish heritage of my father. It was a household infused with passion, artfulness, pathos and humour; interestingly, not the first qualities in the parenting books! These visceral memories reside in my body and were the beginning of my desire to weave the possibilities of connecting orality, language and expression together in my young heart. Now many years later I can connect these formative experiences to the physicality of language.

In school, I learned to write as all students do. As I learned to write, was I being responsive or responsible? Was a love of writing being instilled in me, or was I being taught to find a way to put the pieces together with the structure of grammar? I learned to write well enough because I got through the ranks of high school, college and graduate school, but I didn't love to write like I loved to spontaneously dance, tell stories, climb rocks, hike, draw, or cook. Writing was a disembodied activity for me and I really never gave the process much thought. It was a necessary task, but not one I adored. How could writing hold the many worlds and emotions which stirred inside my body?

WOMB-STUDIO AND WRITING

In my thirties when I was pregnant with twins, my physician instructed me to stop dancing and teaching and go on bed rest for five months. A difficult task for a very active woman who already had a lively four-year old. The care of my twins in my womb was of the utmost priority, so I followed the instructions of my doctor. As you can imagine, I'm not always good at following instructions. Here I began to listen to my body in a new way – on a deeper level, to the actual beats inside my body. Through that process I came to understand that it was not only important for my babies' health that I get rest, but I and the many parts of me – artist, scholar, and mother – also needed rest. The rest was not just replenishing my physical body, but also my spiritual and emotional bodies. I yearned to be restored from the inside out, and this too was the nature of embodiment. In those months of bed rest I came to call my womb, the womb-studio and began to see all of life as studio space. During this time I was being birthed into a kind of writing that I never experienced before; one steeped in the grammar of the heart.

Once my babies were born, I used their naptimes as times to attend to my own replenishment and creativity. During one of their naps I would also nap. During their other nap I would write. I had one rule: never do any housework, prep for teaching, or domesticities while they napped. Only room for domecstasy! It was a joyful, yet time consuming in the beginning years of raising twins and their older brother. So much was going through me I needed a container to bring my thoughts to the page. Here in the crucible of tiredness, breastfeeding and adjusting to three children I found a refuge in words spilling from my heart to the page. Out of that first year came a book,

In the Womb of God: Creative nurturing for the soul published in 1995. The work on this book eventually led me into my doctoral studies and research in areas of phenomenology and to forge new ways to write through and from the body. These were the beginning lessons for establishing a groundwork to connect the body, language and writing for the years to come.

From this experience, what I came to realize is that I had previously a limited access to my full self when I wrote and during the writing process. Not all words written may find their way to the public, but the discipline of letting words flow onto the page from the heart, breasts, pelvis, chest, belly and every other body part was the practice that taught me to open my whole self. All the rumblings of my bodily perceptions were food for the creative process. I was invited to honour the gamut of everything going through my changing body. Being pregnant and later nursing I could not ignore the presence of my body; the fluctuating hormones had a rise and fall all on their own. The moon was present in my body. Those hormones have been having their own life for decades and the key was to be present to each fluctuation. They were the punctuation of my body and they found their way onto the page.

Once I learned how to more fully engage my embodied experiences and connect to writing I could open up the space for my students to write from the body and see this too as a kind of methodology for reflecting and writing from lived experience. And I don't even like to use that word methodology, since it can be overused in forms of qualitative research and there is no formula to be found, nor is one wanted. I make it sound as if there is a method to this practice. What I'm talking about is a method that is a non-method, a method of being, more than doing.

When I ask undergraduate students as well as most graduate students if they love to write, seldom are hands raise or heads nod. Instead there are contorted facial expressions and comments about writing as a necessary and gruelling endeavour. I've made a mission of my teaching to open up a hospitable space where students can discover writing as organic a process as breathing and as a place of joy. I want writing to be that place where the words are followed as pulses of movements and where the fingers dance. Annie Dillard says it well in her book *The Writing Life*, "The line of words fingers your own heart. It invades arteries, and enters the heart on a flood of breath; it presses the moving rims of thick valves; it palpates the dark muscle strong as horses, feeling for something, it knows not what" (1989, p. 20).

43

RETURNING TO THE BREATH

Breath is the beginning. One of the reasons words get stuck in our heads, is because we have not let breath expand in our bodies. How does one find the exquisite word to baptize a page? Living and writing are inextricably entwined. When we give ourselves full-heartedly, in the body to living, we also open ourselves up to writing in a delicious, fresh approach, where inspiration arrives as wind. Language comes from the physiology of breath and tongue, saliva and sweat. Breathing requires inspiration and expiration and so do our words. We originate from oral cultures. The breathing, sensate body where words leap from the feet to throat is our inheritance as human beings and one, which calls us back home.

The twenty-first century has been informed by technology and there is an emphasis on writing coming from the head, as if it is all up there in the brain and the brain is not part of the body. The thinking body is the thinking brain and wants to inspire and invite you to get your feet in your thinking and your thinking in your feet. How can we claim back the inheritance and connection of oral culture to literary culture? How can we nourish a writing, which comes from the body, where there is a singing and dancing of the world through our words, where words are given the qualities of rhythm and tone and an extension of our innermost core? These are questions I continue to live into.

Years ago, in school, learning and practicing cursive writing were part of children's skill that was learned as part of reading, math, science or art curriculum. Cursive writing allowed for a flow of writing that printing does not contain. Part of my own writing practice is to write by hand and in cursive. I encourage all my students – undergraduate and graduate to keep a practice of writing by hand. I see it as blood transforming into ink. The way the hand moves across the page is a different physical action than fingers to a keyboard. Through the different processes, different syllables, words and ideas emerge. This is a warm-up for the muscles like playing notes on the scale. Small practices offer small beauties. In tiny morsels of action brilliance is honed.

Here's a practice I give to my students for you to try. Write in a continuous flow, keep your pen on the page for a timed period. Do this flow writing several times a week, if not every day. To start, try 10–20 minutes, just write. Write your mess. Write your wonder. Write your questions. Write. No judgment. Let your monkey mind come to the page. Write from your monkey body. Let the page embrace everything running through your mind and body. The mind that does not turn off lets the page be a beautiful embrace of everything running through. We have so much going on in our heads, so much stimuli we are exposed to, that writing with no expectations is like having a good bowel movement! One just gets too clogged up. It's like having your vegetables and fibre for writing. And then when the time to really write is given, words one might have never imagined come to form on the page. There is room in the body to write, to dream, and to let the breath in.

This is a project about remembering our bodies back to ourselves in all we do and be. Writing is part of this project and foremost the breath is asking to reinhabit all of our beings. Any movement practice, whether it is yoga or dance, Pilates or Alexander technique, flamenco or opera, relies on the breath. The breath to inhabit not only our lungs, but also our ribs and back and breathe deeply. Tension is released in the breath, and breath unites our body to our thinking. Returning to the breath allows for a returning to inspiration; to dwell in the place where words come into being. A time to bring our bodies and our breath back into writing. When I teach a class, I always include both writing and movement while also attending to the breath. Even the simple act of sighing can bring attention to be the present. I have learned this – that if I attend to my breath I cultivate creativity in living. I invite you to attend to your breath throughout your days whether at play or work. When you write, begin your writing practice with breathing or even sighing. There are as many ways to breathe as there are to write. Let our words breathe onto the page.

WALKING INTO WRITING

The life-force, energy, eros, god, spirit or however you're comfortable referring to it breathes through all of creation. We are breathing creation and creation is breathing us. For the last few decades, my own practice of writing has been deeply connected to walking. As a kinaesthetic person, I have found that walking roots me to my breath and empties my mind, so I can be open to the blank page. There is a long held walking practice by many writers including Wallace Stevens, Henry David Thoreau, J.K. Rowling and the poet Taneda Santoka. As a guide to my walking and writing, I take philosopher Helene Cixous' words, "Writing is not arriving; most of the time it's not arriving. One must go on foot, with the body" (1993, p. 65). Through my walks I have heard the words, which formed their way into poems, essays, books and performances. The practice of walking a half hour a day, followed by writing in my journal for 20 minutes afterward, has become my go-to, hour-long practice used to warm-up the ligaments, tissues and joints to foster words to come as they may.

I incorporate physical activity and walking in all my classes in order to forge the connections between physicality and literacy in my students. Heightening the capacity to dwell in the sensate world is part of the writing process. Being wide-awake to everything is the breath that forms ideas to the page. Life is faithful to give us many experiences that enable us to connect to our breath and writing. Whether you get out of breath, or intentionally breathe slowly, reminders of connecting breath to bone take place throughout the day. Seldom do we see the relationship between breath and thinking or breath and writing. This book is an invitation for you to consider ways to honour the breath into a visceral creativity. Breath connects to flow. And flow is crucial for artists, writers, dancers, philosophers and scientists (See Csikszentmihalyi, M., 2008).

LAMENT AND WRITING

Flow is perhaps more evident when a human being is grieving. The grieving process cannot be stopped; the flow has its own internal rhythm and map. You and I have had our share of loss, burying beloveds or going through a divorce or an illness. I noticed as I grieved, my breath altered the syllables I wrote. Filling journals with both tears and ink, I wrote my way through each loss. Only a few chapters of hundreds of pages made it to print, but that is not what is important. What has been profound is to let my tears infuse the ink on the page. I wrote to honour each nuance of sadness, to allow it a voice and to find its way to form.

I sometimes wonder if by not grieving one can literally get sick. Tears logistically have toxins that are let out of the system and what happens to the tears one cannot cry. Many years ago, one of my sons, when young asked me, "Mom, what does it look like when a man cries?" I have often thought of that statement, as some cultures do not honour the tears of humans, and particularly those of boys and men. Now there is more room for grief, but there was a time, and still today as well where one should, "just get over it." But one doesn't get over it; one moves through these deep feelings, where even words are not enough to convey.

Our tears are our prayers, the dance of knowing we have loved deeply. This is how we are all interconnected, beyond any language, culture, religion or socioeconomic status. We are born in the threads of loss and laughter, both result in the shape of tears. And both give voice to the page. If we are to be truly wide-awake, as philosopher Maxine Greene (1995) reminds us we must be wide-awake to all; there can be no differentiation between what we are called to be wide- awake to. In this way, we viscerally enter empathy and compassion.

Ancient Yearning

We are the language of stars
torsos spinning in light
primal songs
reside in our flesh

Commune with the infinite
underbelly of the heart
let what we long for
come to the surface

Trees and tears are prayers
creation resides within us
ancient beginnings
yearning for home.

Writing has the capacity to be the container for grief, holding our tears as a beloved. If we let ourselves not be censored, and just write, the page holds the capacity to let each stage of grief, no matter how convoluted it can be to let what has no words, be given voice.

MOVEMENT AND WRITING

For the last two decades, I have taught a course on Embodiment and Curriculum Inquiry, which has now been integrated into several graduate cohorts including Arts Education, Health Education and Active Living and Contemplative Inquiry. Through the teaching of this course across disciplines, I have noticed a hunger to find ways to expand the experience and knowledge of learning, writing and teaching through the body. Over the years I have been able to integrate practices of walking, kayaking, hiking, dancing, playing, stretching and artmaking with writing. I give lots of opportunities to juxtapose physical practices and writing and it has been utterly amazing over the years the stunning work that has emerged from these classes. My students all have big lives and loves and are passionate about areas of research. They have full-time jobs, families and lots of responsibilities while pursuing graduate studies, whether it is Masters or Doctoral work. These small practices exploring the body through movement and writing have become a mainstay of what truly animates their creative, scholarly, and vocational lives as they develop their inquiries or research into a thesis or dissertation. Most importantly, I witness them incorporating these practices into their daily lives.

I encourage my students to find a physical practice that connects to their life and to write from that experience. The physical practice could be running or cooking, yoga or tennis, painting or swimming. The practice is to allow time to go into the flow and the energy in the body where one literally writes from and through the body. There is never one way; there are many ways. You must do what truly works for your schedule and life. For example, my own walking practice began because I could not go to dance classes or meditate quietly while raising three children and working full time. Walking was accessible to me. After a while my walking became a dance and flow where everything was walking, and everything was writing. Being, walking and writing became inextricably connected. The flow of life was one big spiral beckoning me to its source, to drink from the source, and write from the source. To dwell in the place where I was tied into an energy much larger than myself and my own petty issues of what to cook for dinner or how to pay my bills.

GETTING UNSTUCK

I have had the joy over the last many years to work with hundreds of students midwifing the process of developing their theses and dissertations. I've had ample experience with getting stuck in my own writing and I've worked with many students who've also experienced the process of getting stuck in their writing. One of the ways I've found to get unstuck is to MOVE. Walk around the block, clean the house, dance in the living room, stretch and sigh, or go do something completely different. While your moving, listen! Writer, Natalie Goldberg says, "Writing, too, is ninety percent listening. You listen so deeply to the space around you that it fills you, and when you write, it pours out of you" (1986, p. 52).

It can work wonders to play with the cat, or ride the bus, or do an errand, as the sentences you are struggling with will find their way to the page. Moving the body is moving words. Syllables need space to dance just as the birds need the sky to soar. Birds teach me to write and to be like everything else does. They soar and glide in a way, which is seamless across the sky outside my condo. I have taken to even watching the crows outside my window in the morning with coffee. They may be a nuisance to some, but I have found my way into their beauty and I am learning from these black creatures of the day. The following poem I wrote speaks of the way they open me to being wide-awake.

Crowdance

What do the black creatures
think in sunbathed early sky?
creation is their stage
working river their prop
background for jubilance
pink orange drapes your tiny bodies

Levity is the main paragraph
you cut through grammar
with sentences of flight
to soar is your verb

You are the preface
to morning rush and rise
crowdance on the Fraser

Why isn't the whole neighbourhood
on their patios with coffee
watching the show?
nature's performance artists
calling us to wake

The birds call me to wake and call me to want to bring words to the page as they glide through the air. Said so beautifully by Terry Tempest Williams:

Once upon a time, when women were birds, there was the simple understanding that to sing at dawn and to sing at dusk was to heal the world through joy. The birds still remember what we have forgotten, that the world is meant to be celebrated. (2012, p. 205)

I have often spoken of the capacity for us to listen to what beats in our hearts, whether it is joy or lament. And our joy holds the jewel to give us deep guidance. Joy has a visceral quality, tangible in its texture. Where our joy is, will be where our words reside. Where our grief is will be where our words reside. In these places, and the ones in-between are the great canvas for the birthing of what we will give birth to in the world.

WRITING FROM OUR VULNERABILITIES

Vulnerability often reveals itself through our bodies; the tension in the shoulder, the butterflies in bellies or heartache in the chest. There is no absolute map to the places where one opens up to fragility or vulnerability. Yet this is what makes us human, what deeply connects us to each other. I have never been one of those people who could separate my personal and professional life. Since I deeply believe in the connection between them, it is my practice to integrate everything running through my life onto the page. Vulnerability comes from the word, *vulnere,* which means to tear open. I have thought many times, of philosopher Luce Irigarary's words, "a wound may create the sky" (1992, p. 84). As much as we may want to control our lives, there are often no ways one could predict the kind of losses or mishaps one will experience. Every day there is unpredictability greeting us whether it is cancer, war, terror, loss, the birth of a child or a creative act. Loss cannot be planned, but it can be transformed if allowed to breathe into being. I will never forget the day that I was just about to go into teach my class in Movement Education and the two planes had crashed into the buildings in NYC during 911. I changed what I was doing that evening for class, and we explored what it meant to integrate grief and our bodies; dancing our fears, shock, grief and honouring what cannot be captured in words.

There is a certain kind of texture where fragility lies. As difficult as it is, there is a brittle beauty to the branches that are dying or the leaf crumbling, or a season of life shifting. Recently I was at a retreat in New Mexico. We were invited to go outside and create on the grounds and I was drawn to dance in the orchard where I found limbs of trees in between life and death. Here I found a kind of liminal space to move amidst the trees' arms, and my arms became an extension of where its branches lay. I am reminded of Tagore, the great Indian poet and philosopher's poetic line that says, "Be still my heart these great trees are prayers" (1997, p. 6). The landscape echoed my own inner landscape calling forth to create from my own fragility. Not to escape it, or wash over it, but to dance and move through it. This of course became the material for my writing.

It is not as important what you "produce," but the textures of vulnerability are encouraged to have room in all creative processes. When I was in my early thirties both of my parents died within eight months. Newly moved to Saskatchewan, Canada and an only child, my devastation took form in dancing my grief in my basement each day, when there was no separation from my tears and the rips in my soul. Lament took shape in the contractions deep within. None of those dances or writings came to light till many years later, when I wove the material into performances and books, but my own practice allowed me to feel comfortable with opening up the space for others to let their grief be a source of expression and a portal to integrate their tears into ink. Writing has the capacity to be the container for our vulnerabilities and the shadow parts of ourselves. If we let ourselves not be censored, and fall into our own gravity, and just write or dance, the page and floor will hold the capacity to let each stage of life, no matter how convoluted, to let what has no words, be given voice. I am reminded of the poet Rilke's words (in Barrows & Macy, 2005, p. 17).

> this is what the things can teach us:
> to fall, patiently to trust our heaviness
> Even a bird has to do that
> before he can fly.

As a dancer, I know how to fall. We are trained how to fall in contemporary dance, letting our bodies fold into the ground and make friends with gravity. Here in the fragility is strength, giving into grace. I invite you to fall into both the fragility and strength and here is the terrain of the fruitful dark.

Writing from the body gives you opportunity to honour each subtle and bold sensation of life; to respond to the world and ourselves. Therefore everything is material for writing and listening to our lives and the grammar of our own lived experience. We don't have to go on an exotic trip to excavate the inspiration for researching our lives. It is right in front of us, with us, and before us. It's all in the prepositions. Our task is to listen and honour everything and see the beauty in small things as well as big things. This beauty may be dissonant, yet it holds the infinite in the palm of our hands. So I invite you to hold it gently, caress the details of your own life and let the shape come forth.

BODYPSALM FOR WRITING FROM THE BODY

Call back your body to the page
the pulse, breath and passion
residing in your cells
sitting on your skin
waiting to come forth
from pores to words

Know each sensation
is syllables of the belly
even agitation is a comma
each heartbeat is the rhythm
yearning to articulate
through the muscles of your fingers

Let physicality take you
to the studio within
where stories are ancient and primal
and love them all into being
here lies the hymns of your body
pronouncing themselves
to respect each flutter and fragrance
of your senses

This is more than common sense
but body sense
the paints for your canvas
notes for your song
movements for your dance
bold creation awaits
you are your body
and your body wants a voice.

There is an art to listening to our lives.
Research is not only an outward endeavour,
but it travels in the realm of re-searching
our own lives, knowledge, passions and practice.

Snowber, "The Mentor as Artist: A poetic exploration of listening, creating,
and mentoring". *Mentoring and tutoring: Partnership in learning.*
(2005, p. 346)

Creativity waits at our gate, breaks into the cracks, in the openings,
where one thinks it will not be, and says, "listen," "see," "behold."
I am here. I am in the absences. I am in the presences.

Snowber, *Visceral Creativity.* (2013, p. 260)

LISTENING AND THE BODY

live with soul and spine
attend to body wisdom
step into the shifts

Listening calls to the canopy of our senses. Our ears hear, so does the heart. The entire body hears. I listen to the light as I feel its softness on my skin. I listen to the ache within me noticing a longing within. I listen to the stiffness in my shoulders; they tell me it is time to swim again. Listening is not only about getting the tasks of life done. I listen to the joy calling me back to what truly matters in my life.

How does one listen? It is not just an activity of the mind, but everything within us: mind, heart, body, soul, imagination and cognition. Or one could say it is fingers, toes, pelvis, hips, neck, breath and shoulders. Listening to the body is one of the greatest gifts we are given as humans. Listening is hearing the bold proclamations and subtle sensations.

Twenty-four years ago today I listened to the movement of my womb, where two babies were moving around wanting to be born into the world. When one is pregnant with twins, one must pay attention. You can't just say, "I'll attend to that task now," for when the birth is coming, it is coming. I did not give birth, but birth came through me. A loud announcement to pay attention to what was happening in my body. Sometimes our birthings are not so dramatic, and are harder to pay attention to. It is truly an artform to listen to the subtleties in our lives; how we respond and react to our own inner knowing. There are many distractions of listening to outside noises, whether it be trains or tractors, televisions or typing; there is an inner listening to what happens within which beckons us to attention. This is not attention, where one is upright and solid, but a soft attention that wants to transform into an exquisite listening. Where listening is expanded to hearing the vibrations beneath the sounds, and with the sounds of our hearts.

LISTENING AND THE SENSES

Listening to and through the body is a daily and ongoing practice. I wish I could say that I always listen to my body and follow its wisdom. I don't. I don't always trust or act on my gut. However, when I reflect back, I wonder why I didn't trust what my belly was saying. Listening to my body doesn't always make sense in the moment, but it is rooted in the senses. The senses that are known through the six senses link to the sense beyond. One can call it many things; whether it is intuition, spiritual, psychic, but there is always a way beyond our own understandings. Wisdom lies here waiting for us to pay attention. Our body wisdom is paramount here. My own impatience or sense of timing gets in the way.

How do we say yes to what is unseen, but felt through our bodies? What is it that makes us distrust the body's knowing? I have come to understand that I don't listen because I want to avoid pain. I may want the relationship to work out, and not listen to what is not completely healthy about it. Or I may stay in the job that is not life-giving because I'm afraid that there are no other possibilities. Or I may want to approach a person for a conversation, but don't because I'm tentative about any conflict that could emerge. I offer you hundreds of reasons why I stop listening deeply to my body. What I notice is that they typically have something to do with fear. It is when I don't listen that I'm in fear and cut off from the wonder of what can emerge.

Listening happens through our senses and is central to the creative process. Whether I am writing, dancing, cooking, parenting, mentoring or teaching I am listening. When I am listening I notice new ideas emerge and keep my life filled with vitality. If I cooked only by recipe, I would never come up with a new dish. If I went only by information in the parenting books, I'd not be prepared for what the books don't discuss. If we are listening we're in congruence with life's plan. The body wants to be included in the plan along with the mind and heart.

Mindfulness has become part of many disciplines and is now part of school curriculums, support groups, therapy, and even economics. However, I am always curious how our words form our philosophy and why has it never been called, "bodyfulness?" Where is the body in mindfulness; is it only about the mind, or can there be a way of including the body into deep attention? I invite you to bring the body to what it means to be deeply attentive. The body is not always neat and tidy. The body has edges and is messy, for we leak, spill, change and rearrange our blood cells everyday, not to mention we urinate and vomit, and have orgasms, all which include the loss of fluid. The body

is the glorious impossible and is the place of knowledge and wisdom – the
great love story.

the great love story

art is a faithful lover
wooing you back each time
the mistletoe of life
begging for a kiss
calling forth your attention

art always waits to be
caressed, loved into being
imagination is the foreplay
union with the creative force
asks no more than this –

make me
play with me
put my skin on
dwell in my terrain
a playground for the body and soul
fingers and hips
words and notes

taste the juice of creation
let go of any expectations
where I will take you
and prance with abandon
I can be trusted
and will not disappoint
always wait for you
as a patient lover
seeking to be born
over and over again.
through your flesh
in your cells
with your tissues

You never know
what I will bring
and when the surprises
of disruption and birth
will be announced in your life

This is not a clean
straightforward path
but a spiral geography
turning from one curve
to another ~ radical spurts
of joy spiced with tears
will moisten the raw canvas of creating

So take your pen and paintbrush
hands, feet, voice and belly
and let me slow dance with you
to form the visible – the audible
from the invisible
and know this
artmaking
is the great love story.

THE BODY AS MUSE

The body is a precious habitat. There is a way of being towards our bodies. One that is about the felt body; how one experiences energy running through the body. The body is asking to be listened to, to be heard.

This listening isn't just between ourselves and our bodies, but it is body to body, earth to earth, earth to body, and to what is beyond. There is a long history of muses to inspire artists and writers, dancers and poets, scientists and seekers. I'm a bit of a practical kind of gal, but live in between the zones of spirit and the physical. I'm after the muse in daily life. I yearn for dailiness to be extraordinary and I admit I'm a junkie for epiphanies and a doorway to grace. Grace comes when we least expect it. I want to be surprised and jolted out of my own perpetual habits of being, thinking or planning. Inspiration not only comes to spirit, but to body, to bodyspirit, to bodysoul. The etymology of the word muse is to "literally stand with one's nose in the air," or to "sniff about." This is so telling because truly we need to be in an open stance to sniff out divine inspiration. To sniff out the beauty in the midst of terror. One may not go walking around the neighbourhood with the nose literally in the air, but one can make available the full self to be in a state of openness and alertness for when the muse will come. Practices which honour the connection to body and mind, heart and emotions, kidneys and kisses, are all valuable. Break open into the wildness that dwells in the wilderness of your bodies.

Your body is a riparian zone, waiting on the edge for something rich and textured to break through. Feed and nourish and honour everything within you. I am reminded what Jesus said in the Gospel of Thomas (in M. Meyer, Trans., 1986, p. 32).

Jesus said,
"If you bring forth what is within you,
what you have will save you.
If you do not have that within you,
what you do not have within you will
kill you."

This statement has many layers of meaning, but what is within you, includes all your senses and opens one up to the senses, which defy order, and break open to mystery. Perhaps the muse is one's relationship to one's body.

LISTENING TO OUR PASSION

I often teach students going back to do masters or doctoral work. I find these students tend to be in a place in their lives and careers where they listen to the call of their own of passions. These calls are what has guided them to find their interests and places for new beginnings. I notice undergraduate students are often at the beginning of their exploration; they are often more connected to what they are suppose to do. I ask them two questions at the beginning of their semester. What is an individual passion in their lives? and what is their major or interest in university? Seldom is there a relationship between what they are passionate about and what they are studying. I find this remarkable and invite them to write about this (dis)connection. Over the semester, as they practice embodied ways of knowing, learning and experiencing, a path to the articulation of their own voices opens. To be given permission is a place to honour the body.

Our passions reside in the body. There is too little time on this planet to not pursue what one is deeply called to. Thriving asks for us to listen to joy and sorrow. I firmly believe that in a world where we have the possibilities to thrive beyond survival there can be what I call *surthrival*. Not just surviving, but thriving. Here in the listening are clues hidden for how one can bring meaning to one's own world and to the larger community.

To listen to one's own passion is to listen deeply within the body. The most important thing you can do is to show up for your life. You have a unique part to play in the world. To be an improviser, one is catapulted into the magnificent present. To show up for your lives you need everything – your whole body, mind, heart, pelvis, fingers and knees!

We are called to listening to the body over and over again. I continue to do this practice because I am hindered as you are. Coming from a performance and dance background can be brutal in terms of dealing with perfectionism and body-image. Accepting the limitations and beauties of the body at the same time is a lifetime practice.

LISTENING AND INSIGHT

I am after not only sight, but also insight. What happens within the sight, within the hearing? I wonder why it should not be called *inhear* instead of insight, since often when one gets guidance, deeper understanding, epiphanies there is a kind of inner hearing. I have an ongoing curiosity about how to make myself more available to insight, inspiration, divine understanding, spirit or the numinous. I have had my own circuitous journey into spirituality through various traditions. I have a deep sense of the Beloved walking with me in my life. As I look back over the times that became most profound, I realize they occurred when I got out of the way. Perhaps that is why when we are dreaming, there is room for the great mystery to unfold through our beings and it can be years till one deciphers the magnitude of a dream.

So I would invite you as I invite myself to consider that the materiality of our bodies is actually the place for the spiritual to take root. Here we become available to the rivers of insight which may want to come into our lives. This is not something we can control, manufacture, or manifest on command. What we can do is cultivate a state of openness, a place of fertility.

As I write this, the morning is still bringing its presence into the sky. Light is arriving gently over the mountains. My cat snuggles up on the couch and I have my dark coffee in hand. I cannot order the sunrise, but I can be present to its arrival. Presence is all we are asked. To listen to presence, to be present is to be in a place of alertness and awakeness. To deeply attend with all of our selves, with each cell and fibre of our bodies, with the wide-open heart is to stand in awakeness.

There are not rational explanations for when or why deep insight comes. I know for myself it often comes when I am walking. While in motion I can hear the voice of spirit, the voice of mystery, goddess and god. Often there is a humour in the truth.

Several years ago I was taking my daily walk around the coastal inlet of water I have walked for decades near my home. At that time, I heard a voice break into my contemplative walk. I was just minding my own business and none other than my dear father, long ago passed away, spoke to me in his New York accent about dating on-line. He said, "You've heard about arranged marriages, right? Well, I'm going to do an arranged marriage from the other side." He instructed me to get my hands off of dating, and just surrender to my beautiful life and do nothing. This also came after I created a whole full-length show including dance and comedy, called, "Woman giving birth to a red pepper," which explored themes of dating, mid-life and sexuality. Then my father proceeded to tell me that the reason he was telling me this here was because was because he always loved the birds and the birds were here in this place. I do not know how to explain any of this in a scientific way, nor do I feel I need to. What I know is that my father's words broke open to me in my walking, and eventually an amazing man was brought into my life a few years later. We are now married, and continue to find the most exquisite ease in being together. I was just in the rhythm of my limbs, walking the path and there came insight. Interrupted by insight informed my choices of doing nothing. And in doing nothing, what I deeply yearned for arrived.

Insight or *inhearing* comes in many forms. As simple as a flash in the heart or an epiphany while swimming, or a gut feeling in one's stomach. It is time to pay attention. Let us listen to every morsel of knowledge and wisdom and surrender to what wants to run through us.

BODYPSALM FOR LISTENING

There are habitats beyond
the one you live in
beneath you in the magma
beside you in the wind
inside you in dreams

layers exist within the archaeology
of your body's knowing
it only takes a drop
of insight to remember
there is another way

where the answer to issues
is not another meeting
change of direction, drive or data
but a realignment to the inward pool
listening through the body
an intuitive's call

the researcher may look for data
but there is a data of the body
spiritsongs of the cells
beckoning you to come alive

turn towards the threshold
of muscles and tissues
let light in the shadows
break into humility
and embrace beyond
what is known.

There is a need to befriend the body
back to ourselves…
There is an unborn song within all of us,
waiting to be born.

Snowber, *Dancing a Curriculum of Hope: Cultivating Passion as an Embodied Inquiry.* (2012b, p. 122)

I am therefore more and more invited into what it means
to "not know" rather than "to know."
The more I delve into fleshing inquiry through the body,
the more deeply aware I am of the paradoxes within me.

Snowber, *Bodydance.* (2002, p. 31)

THE BODY AND PARADOX

> earth bares the body
> gravity and levity
> salting our lives

We live between the juxtaposition of gravity and levity. Gravity roots us to the earth, we take flight in levity. What roots us to difficulty and vulnerability also opens us up to beauty and wonder. Strength and fragility go hand in hand, foot to foot. The irony of many athletes and dancers is they can develop one injury after another, particularly as they age and yet still have much to offer. The pursuit of excellence and strength breaks open the way for the limitations of the body. What is often seen as limitation is actually the place of generativity. Whether it is seeing our injuries as a place of possibility, or our grief as a source of compassion and place to access our humanity, the paradoxes within our lives give rise to the depths.

GRAVITY AND LEVITY

I keep returning to what it means to grieve because we all experience it on the planet and lament is rooted in the body. When we cry, it is our whole body that heaves, the shoulders, eyes, cheeks, and heart are physically responding to the loss. Even if we may not have a deep belly cry, the water within us comes through. Connecting to our tears is the place of honouring our deep humanness rooted in the humility of humus. Humour and humus and humility all woven as a three-strand chord. Tears are prayers, the yearning of our bodyselves calling out to be heard and named.

How do we listen to the parts of our bodies which don't often have voice in our culture? I am often intrigued how other cultures have places of lament, walls to wail at, colours to wear, rituals which honour mourning. But often in Western culture we need to get over it. A few weeks after a death we are expected to be done with grief. When the reality is that it may take years and months and days, with no linear path to the cycle of grief. I have danced grief in my body for years as a way of working out the loss and anguish of losing both my parents in eight months as a thirty-year old, where the contractions of my body and movements on the floor were places for lament to have a home. It is only after years of dancing spontaneously the gut-wrenching grief, did I start incorporating the connections between dance and grief and was able to access the full spectrum through my body and integrate into other performances. So when a student tells me he or she may have to leave during the semester and not finish the major assignment, I invite them into seeing grief as their inquiry. Here is where one can archive what the body has to teach. And inevitably the profound place of learning and honour comes forward to be a discovery of gems. Honour the tears and here is a place of both gravity and levity.

Nowhere have I learned more about the importance of paradox in the body than from my own injuries. I have come to understand my injuries and limitations as places of possibility. For instance, I have created dances on chairs when my knee had surgery. The chair became not only my support, but also a partner in the dance, a place to create a piece, which shifted my own movement vocabulary and emerged a way of theorizing the relationship between limits and possibilities. I found a way to dance beyond the span of my limbs (Snowber & Gerofsky, 1998). This limitation or limit could be seen as a threshold. A place for new movement language and possibilities to emerge in a way that was not possible with a fully working knee. My discovery process opened up a decade of site-specific performance of integrating trees, stones, rocks connected to land and sea as a support and partner in performance. I now see that there has been a knee wisdom in this long process.

BODY AND THRESHOLDS

A threshold can be a limit and an opening. Thresholds are often seen as liminal spaces and places, where mystery and magic open. Recently, when traveling the Wild Atlantic Way on the west coast of Ireland I was once again rebodied to the threshold of the land, in between the seen and unseen. The spaces of seen and unseen are what all artists and seekers long for, bringing forth the visible from the invisible. This too is important for researchers and inquirers, those seeking knowledge and wisdom from the lived curriculum of our lives and making meaning on this planet. In searching for my Irish roots and the Atlantic Way I felt the land awaited me as a loom for its threads. In this place between roots and mist, I roamed to let place form my writing. To listen to lichen where each stone unfolded its stories and notice what arrives.

In between the syllables

I look for roots
in doors and pathways
a hint of a family name
in a village, city or town in Ireland
Killarney, Rosscommon, Galway
little lies substantial
to follow – a wild chase
with nothing at the end.

What happened to the
stories of the great-great
grandfathers – Campbells & McDermotts
who came at age sixteen
to Brooklyn; time of the potato famine
who was left and what
swirled in their hearts
to leave a country such
as this of stone walls
and ancient sentences rolled
in moss and bog, changing
light in hills and sea

a rough history and a rough ocean
beheld in the terrain where I now journey
and find deep hues of resonance
embrace my sassy nature and wild edge

humour and humus is the ground
of this place, my Irish father's eyes
are caught in the people
as if they were siblings

Roots are beyond the place
and within the place
here is the invisible honoured by the visible
waiting underneath the moist earth
to rebody my yearnings to know

that love lies in the space
in between the syllables
of earth, sea and sky.

I would like to propose that the limits and longing in our bodies are
threshold spaces. Here the syllables of our lives make up the fabric of our
bodysouls. Our ability to feel each nuance can bring subtleties of awareness
to what is yearning within us.

One would think there is needed years of practice in yoga or meditation,
and this too is precious, but perhaps there is a way to have a yoga of limits
and thresholds; paying attention to each limit with all our breath and
attention. We carry a yoga room inside our bodies. We are the yoga mat. All
is needed is to be totally present and make friends with our bodies. This may
sound simple, but I am an advocate of engaging in practices that support the
body heart, body mind connection. Whether it is kayaking, singing, walking,
cooking, dancing, making love, sleeping, writing or painting, all involve the
connection to body and mind. But I invite you to see your bodies as a place
where you can search and research what you deeply know within you. The
body is a site of inquiry, a place that is on the threshold of possibility. Even
our longings and yearnings are located inside our bodies which are places
to uncover new ways of being. Nothing is changing as much as our bodies.
Aging is a continual process of change, yet many of us don't embrace these
changes since it is equated with loss. But I would propose the change is a
sacred space to see the body as a place of deep ongoing learning.

KNEE WISDOM

Our bodies often invite us into compassion. The body has its own clock,
radically different than any schedules we have designed. No times are
more poignant for disrupting our busy agendas than sickness, surgery, grief
or injury. This was never more powerful to me than when I thought I was
listening to my body during my recuperation from a knee replacement. I
made a career out of forging ahead in immense difficulty. I learned how to
do this as I raised my sons as a single parent, as I went through the tenure
process, and as I danced on chairs before surgery. I am a fighter, coming
natural to me, as my mother is a survivor of the Armenian genocide. In my
fight to recuperate, I had overdone it with the rehab exercises. I even made a
dance out of these exercises in a limited way, adding ballet arms and Baroque
music as I sat in my chair and bent my knee hundreds of times. As a dancer

with injuries still performing in her late fifties, I knew how to breathe through the pain and make slow progress, although the slow I wasn't very skilled at; patience is not my virtue, but self-discipline is a terrain of familiar territory. I persisted as if doing a marathon and to my dismay at six weeks recovery I developed a Baker's cyst and could hardly move from the pain. By the time I got into the surgeon the following week the first thing he said was, "You have overdone it haven't you?" Of course I sheepishly said yes, but I was confused. I thought I was listening to my body, so good I was at this task. I often say I do this work, not because I'm so embodied, but I need it; to find the body's pace and wisdom and listen to its subtle and bold proclamations. It has been a huge challenge for me to listen to my knee and I am still in the midst of pacing myself and living into compassion for what I can and cannot do. My knee was the receiver to my GPS system within my body. In bold signals, I was called to pay attention. I am continually humbled to learn new rhythms required for healing the parts of our bodies which call out to be heard. Perhaps it is not your knee, but something else; cholesterol or blood pressure, eye or sinus problems, loss through death or divorce. Either way it affects the heart and the word *hear* and *ear* is in heart. We are beckoned to hear the rhythm of our own hearts and limbs and ask what they have to teach us.

They don't send you home from the hospital with a guide on "how to listen to your body," for recovery, health and wholeness. Instead I got a sheet with big, bold, black letters; "Don't eat the frozen peas out of the frozen pea bag." How radical it would have been to have received tips on how to listen to my knee. Bordering on the absurd, I am thankful for small humours. Our bodies are places for listening and guidance, in both their fragility and ecstasy. A natural stopping and pause. There are movements everywhere about SLOW, whether it is slow food, slow culture, or slow sex. Why is it so different to give ourselves permission to slow down to let the body be our guide?

DANCING INTO GUIDANCE

What does it mean to have our bodies give guidance? The word "guidance" has *dance* within it; dancing into guidance, moving into guidance, it is never a static thing. The etymology of the word guidance comes from the Frankish, "show the way." A guide is literally one who shows the way. The body has been given to us as a guide to show us the way. I encourage you to let the body be a source of guidance and direction. The body longs to be a place of discernment for not only our individual lives, but also our collective lives.

Dance with your guide, listen deeply, honour the rumblings and risings, your restlessness and resistance, have compassion on everything you traverse in your lived experience.

You may have heard the expression, "listen to your gut." Have you ever wondered how you actually do that? And where actually does the wisdom reside? Is it in the belly, gut, pelvis, hips, fingers, shoulders or all of the above? I'm inviting you to see all of your body as a place of listening. The gut is your entire body and for each person the locus of listening may be different. What is important is to create practices to hear and honour the body's knowledge. I often invite my undergraduate and graduate students to inhabit their entire bodies, and in particular their hips. Western culture has often forgotten the importance of the hips and pelvis even though every generation wants to be hip. I constantly speak of "pelvic inquiry," and warm-ups in movement include inhabiting the pelvis, hips, and belly and not to think of them as an endangered species. This may feel uncomfortable at first, even comedic, but the pelvis has been waiting to be swung and moved. Of course any dancer or martial artist knows the power in the centre of the torso, but this is information for everyone! A hidden source of endless energy resides within us, it only needs to be honoured and activated. The pelvis, knee or sternum can too be the "listening to the gut." We are interconnected in all of who we are and this is a wonderful time to reclaim both the limitations and possibilities of our whole bodies.

STERNUM TO SKY

The body is not static. Constantly changing, flowing, leaking, recovering, replenishing; the one constant is that bodies are always moving. Even as we are still, there is movement of blood through our cells. Yet in too many lives, movement has been relegated to putting fingers on phones, shoulders and necks slouched down and being more concerned to be connected with a cell phone than the living body. Seldom when walking in the university halls do I see a student walking as if he or she is taking in all the worlds around or being present to the beauty of their own steps. One wonders how many pedestrian accidents will occur because all attention is on technology. The exquisite, complex technology of our own bodies goes unnoticed until something is not working. I sometimes ask my undergraduate students to leave the classroom and wander down the halls and just observe the gestures that are visible around campus. Undoubtedly they are the same. Shoulders hunched over and fingers pressed to the phone texting. I can't believe there wouldn't be a generational issue or consequences in postures of bodies slouched over cell phones. What ever happened to the relationship of sternum to sky, to feel the wind on our skin, to look each other in the eye, or connect our heads to our tails or shoulders to feet?

The fast pace of many of our lives can still foster a paying attention to the body's nuances and allow for deeper alertness through all our being. It only takes a few minutes to stop and touch in with ourselves, do a body check and listen to how our feet are planted on the earth or how we are attending to breath. The sky is calling our sternum to have a chest of expanse and the earth calls our feet to be firmly grounded on the soil. Here lies the paradox of both going through days sometimes not attending to the nuances of our bodies, and letting those moments seep into the viscera. Perhaps the body has been programmed out of listening mode, and its ability to be a guide has been forgotten. This book is a beckoning back the body to be a wise mentor for each of us. The body is an organic spiritual director, waiting as a patient lover does, to return you to what it means to be human.

Instead of being perplexed by the paradox of the body, perhaps it is time to praise it. Paradoxology – in praise of paradox is what the body teaches us.

BODYPSALM FOR LIVING INTO PARADOX

Welcome back to the familiar
the land of the perplexed
where paradox reigns
and heart, mind, and body
are not in sync,
harmony, congruence or flow
and no matter how diligent
you are to reflect,
problem solve, brainstorm or bodystorm
it sits as a big mountain
in front of you
and cannot be climbed with bare feet

you are in the terrain of paradox
the geography of the unknown
where the brittleness of breath
lives amongst the stars
your task is to breathe
deep into the place you are perplexed.

Take shoes for the journey
these aren't any shoes
but these are your dancing shoes
the ones that look like sneakers
but have a support for your arch

Life holds continual
places of dissonance
it doesn't matter the source:
disappointment or sorrows
with relationships, health or finances
Know this: P A R A D O X
will always be there
singing at the door
waiting for you to

Put your dancing shoes on
give yourself the support you need
a bigger arch for life
and treat paradox as your partner
hold it tenderly
romance her and put your
arms around the dilemmas
soften your relationship
towards not knowing.

Breathe into uncertainty
knowing this is the
essence of life
and when it comes
know you are invited
once again into
the spirituality of practice:
loving-kindness towards
all that is not resolved
in your heart.

The geography of the inner life
beckons me through the visible paths
of the natural landscape
and I listen, stop, move and dance.
Walking and dancing become my litany;
the invitation to see and hear again
for the first time.

Snowber, *On the Breath of Limbs.* (2014a, p. 121)

AN ECOLOGY OF THE BODY

body signature
my belly moves to earth's pulse
listen to the land

Our bodies are the earth. The earth is our body. In my practice of walking, dancing and writing in connection to the landscape and seascape I keep living these words. My body is the earth – the earth is my body. At first my practice of walking the edge of a shoreline park at the cusp of land and sea was enough. Here I emptied my busy mind and gave in to the rhythm of my feet to the land and my nostrils to the scents of sea and coniferous woods. My eyes and heart learned from the creatures, which blessed this part of the world: herons and eagles, seals and slugs, bears and seagulls. These were my companions for two decades raising my children on the edge of the wild in the suburbs. In this place, I accessed my own wild heart, one which called out to something larger than myself. The inlet's path hugging the sea became my sanctuary. This was the cathedral where I returned every day with my black lab to find solace, insight and inspiration and to return to the pulse of my own body. Step by step I touched the lifeblood of breath and in return was touched by creation beckoning me to inhabit fully the earth's offering.

DANCING IN THE ALPHABET OF CREATION

Walking was eventually connected to the practices of other forms of artistic expression. Out of these forms came syllables and words forming poems that were site-specific to the landscape. Walking and writing became inextricably linked. I walked. I wrote. The words deep within my belly and breath formed from the rhythm of my feet to soil. I heard another alphabet from the land and sea and took these alphabets to the page. Eventually it was not enough to walk the earth, I had to dance there. Whether walking or dancing the earth, I was in partnership with creation, moving to the pulse of the land and tides of the sea. Hafiz, the 14th c. Persian poet says (in Ladinsky, 2010, p. 152)

There is no spot on earth that ever became sacred until
something danced there; maybe it was just an atom or two.

The inlet became my studio, where creation spoke to me and through me.
The creations from this "studio" took several forms. I created a site-specific
performance of poetry and dance connected to the ecology of this place. I
shared my work with others: undergraduate and graduate classes, the public
and friends. I brought them on an hour and a half contemplative walk in
silence, sharing the poetry and dance emerging out of this site and in turn
asked them to let all their senses be awake to this Pacific Northwest land
which spoke a language all of its own. I was launched into understanding
something very different about the intersections between ecology and the
body through these experiences. Just as climbing my tree as a child changed
my perspective and perception, so did site-specific performative work
transform my relationship to breathing, living and creating. We need to sit at
the earth's feet once again and hear the ache of her land.

WE ARE MADE OF STARS AND SCARS

We are the land. The land is us. We are the water. The water is us. We are
not separate from the earth, but part of it. We are all made up of stars. The
physical world is shot through with the pulse of the holy. We understand this
viscerally, deep in our bones and under our skin, there is a sense that we are
all part of the DNA of the universe. We are all made up of stars. Physicists and
oceanographers speak of such things, and there is much scientific evidence
to corroborate these ideas. I need to know things in my viscera; in the text of
my body. I did not just need evidence. I needed *evidance.* When I danced, I
knew an ancient knowing that I was part of the earth. I am earth.

Have you danced enough under the night sky, at dawn's opening light in
the fields, forest, or on the edge of stone? Indigenous cultures have known
the power of dance outside in creation for time beyond time, but we have
forgotten the ancient wisdom. Theologian and poet, John Donohue wrote,
"When we walk on the earth with reverence, beauty will decide to trust us"
(2004, p. 24). I have let beauty trust me and have taken up dancing in forests,
rivers, beaches, parks and gardens, wherever the natural world calls out to
me. I am fortunate now to be the Artist in Residence in the UBC Botanical
Garden and create site-specific performances of dance and poetry in each
season and share with the public. What started very organically continues to
find a wider place to share these embodied connections to the larger world.

I often wonder how long the plants and flora have been waiting for someone to dance there.

Why is it sanctioned to jog, run, walk, hike, talk, chatter as we walk on the paths of our designated nature trails, but dancing is for fools? We see the leaves dance, the wind dancing, the water dancing, so let us join the dance. Why do we limit ourselves? This is the question I ask over and over to myself and to others. What if we didn't limit ourselves, and let expressivity have its place? Who knows, perhaps the trees are asking for us to salsa on the path, or do creative movement on the sand. Let us dance as children do, playfully inhabiting creation. Creation inhabiting us. Through dance and other forms of movement we come to know the deep truth under our skins that we are not separate, but connected. Where else to understand this but through our bodies?

LIVING FROM SKIN, STONE TO SKY

What I feel in my body, I feel in the earth. There is a crisis of perceiving the earth as something as consumed and used. To begin letting this glorious sensuous earth into your bodies is a place to shift the tides. We are living from skin to sky. The scars of the land are within our bodies. Literally, we bear the consequences of toxicity and pollution, as we bear the glory of feeling the wind in the hair, the moisture on the skin and the fragrance of spring in our nostrils. It is all one. We admire rock, stone, canyon with marks of burnt umber, sienna, charcoal gray and notice the beauty of age. We are attracted to what is worn and ancient. People go from all over the world to find places where stone stands in its majesty. Yet, we do not seem to treasure our own scars, whether they are from accidents, or incisions from operations, or just age. I have always loved the artist, Mary Blaze, whose work who is on the front cover of this book. Her marks are exquisite, bearing the beauty of marks on our bodies. What if we could look at the marks and scars on our aging bodies or young bodies and see the wonder of the canyon lands? Treasuring the fragility and strength as complimentary pairs of being human.

Fleshmarks

You have marks
all over your skin
gradation of pigment

of burnt sienna, burnt
umber, terracotta
clay lavender.

stretch marks
on stone,
beauty squared
infinite tongues
of light.

We don't often treasure
our own marks as yours –
scars, birthmarks
wrinkles of age
but you Canyon
teach us to honour
the marks on our flesh
for they too are
shaped from climbing
into life and here
too is a place
to behold.

RETURNING TO THE EARTH'S INTELLIGENCE

The busyness of our lives on this planet, has made us vulnerable to forgetting. The body remembers and calls us back. Just for a moment, right now, pause in your reading. Remember a place, which called out to you, beckoned to you as a child or even as an adult. Perhaps it is a garden or seascape, or prairie, or a small patch of land in your backyard. It could be one tree. One tree can hold the world. This place is your place of refuge.

Let yourself for a few minutes, find the place you know is the earth's intelligence. Live inside the memory in your body, which may define a sanctuary amidst the natural world. In some small way, invite yourself to return there. What do you smell? What do the sensations within your body feel like? Take a few moments to pause into the preciousness of this place. What calls out to you here? What is it you already know deep in your body? You can go to this same place with your body and mind for retreat.

One of the reasons we don't make time for practice like the one above is that we see them disconnected from our daily work rather than part of it. Being responsive to email is just as important as being responsive to your heartbeat and to the pulse of the natural world. May we not only be responsible, but responsive and let our bodies remember our way back home to the earth. Our body is the earth. The earth is our body.

BODYPSALM FOR THE EARTH

The earth is shaking within its core
and our cores in turn are shaken
now is the season to wake up
from the inside out
proclaim the interconnection
to all living beings –
neighbours near and far
sun, stars, sea, plants and plankton
and most of all
the fertile earth
which both gives and takes away

May we return to humility
where humus, humans and humour are born
and taste the mystery and beauty
beneath our feet and bellies

May our limbs stretch to the sky
our soles/souls kiss the ground
and may hope soak
our minds and bodies
through changes of weather
as we return to the fire of love
which has the capacity
to hold more than we know both of the heart and land

May we bear grace in our bones
and be rebodied to the truth –
our flesh is the earth
and the earth is our flesh

May compassion arise from our well
as we return to the fire of love
which has the capacity
to hold more than we know

My invitation to students, colleagues and myself
is to let out our narratives,
and in particular our body narratives within education,
but always to co-create a better world,
one more human, creative and filled with the possibility
of being more conscious and generative.

Snowber, *Dancing the threshold from personal to universal.* (2014b, p. 2)

BODYWARD

migrate to the life
that wants to be lived in you
one step at a time

The body is not as polite or predictable as us earthlings would like to think it is. As you know we cry, laugh, eliminate, fall, stretch, and sleep, but how the body does these things is not always the same or at the same time. We may like to get seven hours of sleep each night, but it doesn't always work out that way. Interruptions are a given whether it is kids getting up at night, fluctuation of hormones, or the need to empty oneself. I'm sure you can find a series of interruptions from your own sleeping repertoire. When I was going through a period of mourning, I wished I could call a babysitter and say, I'll be crying from 3–4:30, do you think you could come then and watch the kids? Life cannot be predicted; it's not predictable. Life is an improvisation, bringing what follows, a new conversation, idea, and meal – the beauty in the mundane or the holy in the ordinary.

THE BODY IS NOT POLITE

The body is not polite. Yes, the body can be trained, but we are still called to follow the impulses within, I may need to trace the wildness in my own wilderness. I sometimes joke and say even though I have lived in Canada for over thirty years I am still not polite. As I was raised on the East Coast of Massachusetts by an Armenian mother and Irish New Yorker father, interruptions were constant. In some ways interrupting was a way of honouring the conversation, for if you were truly engaged you would interrupt. Conversation was an art accompanied by candles, food, libations, and dancing in between outbursts of laughter, animation and dramatics. However I did find this approach to conversation was not the norm in other households, and as much as I still try to wait my turn and speak at the right time, I hopelessly fail. Our conversations as either a little family or with my extended family or friends were a lively improvisation and performance all to themselves. I look back at them now with deep fondness and wonder if they were the beginning of my training to be an improviser. I refer to myself as a "recovering choreographer" as I have fallen in love with improvisation over the last few decades and I integrate improvisation in all my performance work. It is what is unforeseen within the form that most intrigues me.

Holy irreverence is what I'm after. And it's not polite. To follow the body, one must give up some of the cultural norms, in favour of listening to the rumblings and rhizomes of the body's way. That is a way which has its own path. Courage and trust are necessary ingredients, comprising of falling off the cliff, diving in the water, jumping off the dock, and saying a big YES to the unknown.

what you say yes to

You will be asked over and over again,
"Do you know how to say no?"
as if you have not learned this lesson
over and over again; after all, how do you
think you go through careers, children,
relationships, strangers…you have learned
to say no, but the real question is…

"What do you say yes to? And I am not talking
about all the responsibilities that are on
your shoulders in one form or another.
If you are reading this book you are already
more responsible, which is different than responsive.

Notice
what you say yes to and
how you can say yes MORE to
what gives you life, animates you, feeds you,
nourishes your soul, body, mind, senses, and feet.

So instead of thinking about what you say no to,
be invited to respond to what calls forth to say YES
and here is the place for you to dive in to the unknown.

JUMPING OFF

Letting the unknown be the companion, even befriending the unknown opens you up to surprises, Let yourself be astonished. Ready...Jump!

Here's a story about jumping. When I was growing up in the island town of Nahant outside Boston, Massachusetts there was a dock at the wharf that all of the kids liked to jump off of. I remember an exhilaration when jumping off. You did not know exactly where your body would land in the water; the icy cold water of New England was always there to greet your limbs. Of course it was always more exhilarating to jump off yourself instead of being pushed off and one would arrange a time to just go "jumping off."

Writing, living, being open to the wonders of the body is a jumping off. Courage comes from the word *heart*, denoting the heart as the seat of feelings. The courage of the heart connects to the entire body. This is a visceral courage, a courage to live in the viscera, a courage to be wild and live in one's own wilderness. It is courage to inhabit the spaces of shadow, light and colour no matter what they may be. And to say YES!

DOMECSTACY

There is a time for colouring inside the lines, but a time for colouring outside the lines as well. I ask myself, "what is holding me back? Where are my own resistances, and where am I keeping myself from showing up? I tell my students the most important thing they can do for themselves is to show up, and I tell myself this every day as well. It's a lifelong practice. Otherwise we can get too distracted about what we should do. I don't know about you, but that word "should" can get me into a lot of trouble. I become domesticated by it. It's true, I need to be domesticated enough to pay my bills, put food on the table, or pay attention when driving. There is another kind of domestication that I call "domecstacy." Domecstasy is finding the ecstatic in the daily.

All of the practices in embodied ways of inquiry are about finding the ecstatic in the daily. This is the soil for living into one's own voice. It is the process of rediscovering the passion of honouring our own beautiful lives. There are not formulas or methodologies or research plans to do this. This is the plan that is the nonplan.

We live in a world where almost everything is measured. The academy measures every word I write and evaluates me and my colleagues constantly. I'm asked, is it a top tier journal? Who is the publisher? What is the impact of the piece you wrote and how many times was it quoted? I don't think anyone at my funeral will ask these questions; I hope instead they'll be concerned with the way I loved and laughed and responded to tears. What I am talking about here does not have a measuring stick for it is a listening and attending to your GPS within. Who else but you really knows what direction it gives?

We have all heard – "listen to your gut," "honour your instincts," and yet it seems easier to listen to the messages on our phone or check an email. We are all like a stuffed pepper or eggplant. We are stuffed with a delicious, juicy, beautiful life. If we are too focused on the outside we never get what is within. I want both the stuffing and the outside skin. When I speak to you, I speak to myself. What I say, I say because have to hear it myself over and over again. Let us honour and love every cell of ourselves. That means I love and honour my difficult knees, my changing hormones, my tender heart and my strong will. What do you love and honour about yourself? I live in between a strong and tender place. We are the fragile earth, the fragile body and the strong earth and strong body. The paradox or paradoxology is present. The present to ourselves is to live in the exquisite presence with all of who we are. This is an embodied life. Here, our cells dance.

VISCERAL CREATIVITY

And when our cells dance we allow our body to become a muse. The body becomes a place of inspiration for creativity. This is a visceral creativity; one which lives in our skin and marrow. Here what was not birthed, opens up the possibility for birth. All through the ages, artists have had muses, but I am proposing that our muse is connecting all of who we are: body, soul, mind, imagination and muscles. When there is a deep connection to ourselves, we are radically present and the flow of energy freely moves through us as a symphony. Therefore, it is not only practicing writing, singing, inventing, dancing, but having the practices which sustain us as individuals to bring connections which open up these kinds of ways for radical presence.

In this world, connecting to something, someone or the other is a deep hunger. May we listen to the hunger of connection and give room to foster a sustainable life. Each of us will do this in different ways, but we cannot put it on hold in the backroom. Sometimes it is in the midst of swimming where I truly find inspiration or the ending for a book, or the beginning for a dance. In this flow where each limb gives way to folding into the water my body returns to something far more ancient than sitting at my computer. The primordial rhythm which has held creation holds me and I succumb to another way. This is the way that holds the vowels and syllables to creativity.

And I am folded into astonishment. It didn't take three weeks of a writer's retreat, but a retreat for my body to dive into a rhythm of strokes hitting the water. It may be swimming for me, but it could be walking, fishing or knitting for you. The muse is waiting for us as a patient lover, and perhaps it is not as romantic or ethereal as one would think, but the small practices of making room for the body to be present to the flow of life.

Life is too short to not be absolutely awake. Here is the exquisite place to live deeply into what we each were created for. To find our passion. To live into our passion. To celebrate existence. Even in the midst of difficulty, grief or terror, there is the call to go forward, with all of who we are. Bodyward. Heartward. Soulward. Celebrating the body as a place of inquiry.

BODYPSALM FOR THE REAL

Life is not what it seems
appearances are radically different
than what I S
you hear it said over and over again
it is what it is
what is more important
is
you are here alive
fresh with the naked
vitality of being awake
to the glorious impossible
wrapped in the skin
of a new bud
fresh fallen snow
a glance of love
the boldness of honesty

Dare to be Real
to be who you truly want to be
the time is NOW
for announcing your true heart
n o compromise
in the ground of green earth
n o accommodation
for what you know is not true
stay near to the timbre of your own voice

Find what truly animates
your deepest yearning
and know the closer you live
to your own pulse
the more exquisite you are
for here is your rare beauty
with all your imperfections
let the opposites be present
celebrate blue and orange!

The time is NOW
to live with all your
colours, hues and shades
of the uniqueness of you
Show up for your life
and let the real B E!

REFERENCES

Barrows, A., & Macy, J. (Trans.). (2005). *Rilke's book of hours: Love poems to God.* New York, NY: Riverhead Books.

Cixous, H. (1993). *Three steps on the ladder of writing.* New York, NY: Columbia University Press.

Csikszentmihalyi, M. (2008). *Flow: The psychology of optimal experience.* New York, NY: Harper Perennial Modern Classics. (Original work published 1990)

Dillard, A. (1989). *The writing life.* New York, NY: Harper Perennial.

Goldberg, N. (1986). *Writing down the bones: Freeing the writer within.* Boston, MA: Shambhala.

Greene, M. (1995). *Releasing the imagination: Essays on education, the arts, and social change.* San Francisco, CA: Jossey-Bass.

Heschel, A. J. (2003/1951). *The Sabbath.* Boston, MA: Shambhala.

Irigaray, L. (1992). *Elemental passions* (J. Collie & J. Still, Trans.). London: The Atlone Press.

Ladinsky, D. (Ed.). (2010). *Hafiz: Daily contemplations.* New York, NY: Penguin.

Merton, T. (1961). *New seeds of contemplation.* New York, NY: Directions.

Meyer, M. (Trans.). (1984/1986). *The secret teachings of Jesus: Four gnostic gospels.* New York, NY: Vintage Books.

O'Donohue, J. (2004). *Beauty: The invisible embrace.* New York, NY: Harper Collins.

Snowber, C. (1995). *In the womb of God: Creative nurturing for the soul.* Liguori, MI: Triumph-Liguori.

Snowber, C. (2002). Bodydance: Fleshing soulful inquiry through improvisation. In C. Bagley & M. B. Cancienne (Eds.), *Dancing the data.* New York, NY: Peter Lang.

Snowber, C. (2005). The mentor as artist: A poetic exploration of listening, creating, and mentoring. *Mentoring and Tutoring: Partnership in Learning, 13*(3), 345–353.

Snowber, C. (2011). Let the body out: A love letter to the academy from the body. In E. Malewski & N. Jaramillo (Eds.), *Epistemologies of ignorance in education.* Charlotte, NC: Information Age Publishing.

Snowber, C. (2012a). Dance as a way of knowing. Bodies of knowledge [Special Issue: Bodies of Knowledge: Embodied Learning in Adult Education]. *New Directions for Adult and Continuing Education, 2012*(134), 53–60.

Snowber, C. (2012b). Dancing a curriculum of hope: Cultivating passion as an embodied inquiry. *Journal of Curriculum Theorizing, 28*(2), 118–125.

Snowber, C. (2013). Visceral creativity: Organic creativity in teaching arts/dance education. In J. Piirto (Ed.), *Organic creativity in the classroom: Teaching to intuition in academics and the arts.* Waco, TX: Prufrock Press.

Snowber, C. (2014a). Dancing on the breath of limbs: Embodied inquiry as a place of opening. In A. Williamson, G. Batson, S. Whatley, & R. Weber (Eds.), *Dance, somatics and spiritualities: Contemporary sacred narratives.* Chicago, IL: Intellect, University of Chicago Press.

Snowber, C. (2014b). Dancing the threshold from personal to universal [Special Issue: What docs it mcan to have an N of 1? Art-making, education research and the public good]. *International Journal of Education and the Art, 15*(2). Retrieved from http://ijea.org/v15si2/index.html

REFERENCES

Snowber, C. (2016). *Wild tourist: Instructions to a wild tourist from the divine feminine.* New Westminster, BC: SilverBow Publishing.

Snowber, C., & Gerofsky, S. (1998). Beyond the span of my limbs: Gesture, number and infinity. *Journal of Curriculum Theorizing, 14*(3), 39–48.

Tagore, R. (1997). *The heart of God: Prayers of Rabindranath Tagore* (Selected and edited by H. Vetter). Boston, MA: Tuttle Publishing.

ABOUT THE AUTHOR

Celeste Snowber, Ph.D. is a dancer, writer, poet and educator, who is an Associate Professor in the Faculty of Education at Simon Fraser University outside Vancouver, B.C., Canada. Her essays and poetry have been published extensively in various journals and chapters in books and she is the author of *Embodied Prayer* and co-author of *Landscapes in Aesthetic Education*. Her most recent book of poetry is *Wild Tourist* published in 2016. Celeste has pioneered embodied ways of inquiry within arts-based research and curriculum theory and ways of writing from the body within the academy and is a sought after mentor for graduate students. She is the recipient of the 2016 Ted T. Aoki Award for Distinguished Service in Canadian Curriculum Studies. Celeste continues to create/perform site-specific work in connection to the natural world and has created several performances at the threshold between land and sea. She is presently the Artist in Residence in the UBC Botanical Garden where she is creating performances of dance and poetry in each season. She has also performed a full-length show including dance, humour and voice entitled, "Women giving birth to a red pepper." Her love of improvisation fused with dance and voice takes flight in these performances, which connect the depth, absurdity and beauty of life together. She is the mother of three amazing adult sons and lives with her husband in the Lower Mainland of Vancouver, B.C. Her website can be found at www.celestesnowber.com and blog at www.bodypsalms.com.

Printed in the United States
By Bookmasters